Inclusion, Epistemic Democracy and International Students

"This is an important academic contribution which synthesises a critical perspective on the inclusion of international students in higher education contexts with a careful policy and theoretical critique of the TEF. In this book Aneta Hayes brings together key issues for the higher education sector in the UK and thinks through their implications. She makes an innovative proposal for a new metric based on this critique. This book will be a significant development for higher education studies and a must-read for scholars in policy and higher education."

—Dr. Sylvie Lomer, *University of Manchester, UK*

Aneta Hayes

Inclusion, Epistemic Democracy and International Students

The Teaching Excellence Framework and Education Policy

Aneta Hayes
School of Social Science and Public Policy
Keele University
Keele, Staffordshire, UK

ISBN 978-3-030-11400-8   ISBN 978-3-030-11401-5   (eBook)
https://doi.org/10.1007/978-3-030-11401-5

Library of Congress Control Number: 2018967267

© The Editor(s) (if applicable) and The Author(s) 2019
This work is subject to copyright. All rights are solely and exclusively licensed by the Publisher, whether the whole or part of the material is concerned, specifically the rights of translation, reprinting, reuse of illustrations, recitation, broadcasting, reproduction on microfilms or in any other physical way, and transmission or information storage and retrieval, electronic adaptation, computer software, or by similar or dissimilar methodology now known or hereafter developed.
The use of general descriptive names, registered names, trademarks, service marks, etc. in this publication does not imply, even in the absence of a specific statement, that such names are exempt from the relevant protective laws and regulations and therefore free for general use.
The publisher, the authors, and the editors are safe to assume that the advice and information in this book are believed to be true and accurate at the date of publication. Neither the publisher nor the authors or the editors give a warranty, express or implied, with respect to the material contained herein or for any errors or omissions that may have been made. The publisher remains neutral with regard to jurisdictional claims in published maps and institutional affiliations.

Cover image: © Nikola Spasic/Getty

This Palgrave Macmillan imprint is published by the registered company Springer Nature Switzerland AG
The registered company address is: Gewerbestrasse 11, 6330 Cham, Switzerland

Foreword

International student mobility is one of the most prominent, dynamic and complex phenomenon of higher education in the twenty-first century. The rapid growth of international student mobility has affected the educational, cultural, economic and political discourses of both the sending and receiving countries. It has impacted not only on individual student-sojourners and teachers but also teaching and learning practices, institutional operations and practices across various related fields. International students are considered as one of the primary revenue sources for host institutions, especially in the US, UK and Australia, as three top destinations for international students. In rhetoric, international students are often positioned as valuable members of the classrooms and broader communities in the host countries. Unfortunately, in practice, there has been a systemic hegemony that constructs international students as 'the other', 'subordinator' or 'second class citizen' in the host learning community and broader society. This systemic discourse marginalises international students and leads to their vulnerability in the classroom, at the workplace and in the society. How to challenge this systemic discourse and create the platform to engage with international students on academically, culturally, socially and politically equal terms is central to our effort to make international students feel valued, connected, included and productive members in the host community and thereby optimising their transnational academic and social experiences. It is therefore timely and important that Aneta Hayes explores these issues in her most welcome book, *Inclusion, Epistemic Democracy and International Students: The Teaching Excellence Framework and Education Policy.*

The book makes a distinctive contribution to the growing body of literature on internationalisation and in particular to discussions about policy discourse and inclusion of international students. Aneta's book takes a unique angle to examining the teaching, learning and treatment of international students because it attempts to problematize policies on measuring teaching excellence in higher education in relation to the critical issue of inclusion/exclusion of international students. This represents the first book in the world that focuses on the new and controversial trend of evaluating teaching excellence in higher education and questions its ignorance of the nature and the ways universities engage with international students in the context of increased internationalisation.

The core of this book is made of three parts, which is an excellent combination of theoretical discussions and practical applications. Part I focuses on theoretical discussions of policy as power and how it governs the key issues pertinent to the inclusion of international students. Part II examines the ways policy representations of international students in the UK construct this cohort as culturally and socially subordinated and discusses the ways in which the Teaching Excellence Framework can lead to significant systemic changes. Part III suggests practical implications for the systemic changes that can enable universities to foster more equal, meaningful and productive relationships with international students.

Aneta Hayes's book is a unique contribution to an important field of policy discourse and inclusion of international students. It is likely to be a foundation for much subsequent UK and international work on the ongoing cause of challenging the '*status quo*' of international students as 'inferiors' and eliminating the marginalisation of international students in both policy representations and practices. The book is a comprehensive text analysing policy discourse and suggesting essential steps to engage with international students on academically, culturally and politically equal terms.

Melbourne, Australia
November 2018

Ly Thi Tran
Associate Professor in the School of
Education, Deakin University

Preface

This is a book about international students, exclusion, coloniality in education and so-called 'teaching excellence' policies. It is about the role of these policies in creating conditions for exclusion of cross-border learners. There are two main goals of the book. The first goal is to raise awareness of the ways in which policy constructions can lead to outdated views on international students, and therefore affect developments in internationalisation related to epistemic democracy (understood as equivalence of different geopolitical sources of knowledge and equality of all 'knowers'). Under this goal, the book aims to discuss how, by extension, adequate changes to public policies can revert the damaging effects of these constructions on international students themselves, on home students and university internationalisation more broadly. Through a critical discussion of these changes, the book therefore makes a new theoretical contribution—it is the first book that addresses the question of how the principles of epistemic equality in increasingly internationalised university contexts, understood as freedom to contribute alternative knowledge without fear of coercion and discrimination, can be encouraged at universities through the influence of public policies. The book makes the case that it is imperative that public policies,

ix

especially those related to teaching excellence, mandate that knowledges developed beyond the borders of the nation state are contributed in university classrooms and are given the 'scientific' and 'true' status. The book proposes a radical reform that strives to ensure that principles of epistemic equality and epistemic democracy become constitutive of understandings of excellent teaching. As such, the second goal of the book is to show what practical changes to public policies can be made, so the nations and their universities start considering epistemic democracy as a referent of teaching excellence.

The book focuses on the Teaching Excellence Framework (TEF) as an example of a teaching-related policy that excludes epistemic democracy as a determinant of teaching excellence. The plans for the TEF were introduced in the UK with the publication of the Green Paper *Fulfilling Our Potential: Teaching Excellence, Social Mobility and Student Choice* in November 2015. The framework was later confirmed in the white paper *Success as a Knowledge Economy: Teaching Excellence, Social Mobility and Student Choice* in May 2016. The TEF is thought to signal one of the biggest changes in UK's higher education, shaking up university rankings through transforming ways of evaluating the sector, from criteria related mainly to research outputs to ones that focus on teaching excellence and student outcomes. Many commentators have of course not shied away from criticising the exercise for not measuring teaching excellence, and most analyses in fact agree that the exercise does not do that. But this is not the focus of this book. Rather, the book deconstructs another problem with the TEF—namely the absence of metrics and any discussions about how the TEF, said by its creators to be a major higher education reform concerned with teaching, could change the subordinated position of international students in UK universities. The book also notes a similar problem with the TEF's European and US equivalents, the Assessment of Higher Education Learning Outcomes (AHELO), Measuring and Comparing Achievements of Learning Outcomes in Higher Education in Europe (CALOHEE) and the Collegiate Learning Assessment (CLA). It questions why this is the case and provides some answers. The reflections and the model for a TEF metric on internationalisation that is proposed in the book is also timely for Australia, where preparations are now taking place to introduce an

Australian version of the TEF. Similarly to the TEF, the Australian version intends to measure universities' completion and attrition rates, students and employer satisfaction, employment outcomes and share of students from disadvantaged backgrounds (Ross, 2018). The Australian plans however, just as the TEF and its European and US equivalents, do not include any objectives to evaluate internationalisation.

So this is also a book about ideas: ideas about how the TEF and its European, US and Australian equivalents *could* foster and sustain realisation of international students as democratic equals in university classrooms. These are the ideas that should define the character of teaching at universities of our age and the nature and scope of any national and supra-national frameworks that attempt to evaluate excellence of teaching in the context of increased internationalisation of higher education. Internationalisation, understood as the growth of universities that enter into new social and educational interdependencies with international people (here mainly students), which should prompt social changes that accept these people as democratic equals, is changing our universities. It is no longer marginal and ad hoc, but central—it has revolutionised the national character of our universities. At the same time, university's long connection to the nation state and to imperialism (as it is the case in many Anglophone universities) is an ideological 'threat' to internationalisation because it brings a deep tension between nationalism and cosmopolitanism. Consequently, this tension makes us colonised in mind and practice. Additionally, 'common good' discourses that underlie the connection to the nation state, in the sense of contributing to people's agency (e.g. their civic development, social empowerment and social welfare) never include international students—as if those students were a threat to this welfare. Thus, frameworks that attempt to measure the quality of teaching and student outcomes should therefore take account of how universities respond to this change. Presently, as the book will show, the philosophical basis and metrics underlying these frameworks are drifting away from such core ideas.

Consequently, the book argues that the TEF and its equivalents around the world must be conceptualised in a new way. It offers a new idea for the TEF—that is, as an exercise that should be conceptualised, inter alia, as a tool for fostering epistemic democracy. It is argued in the

xii   Preface

book that this means not only working towards greater equivalence of international students but also doing so in a way that will simultaneously contribute to the democratic life of home students. Such situation, and an effort towards achieving it, is captured and explained in this book under theorisations about "Institutional Epistemic Justice", whereby it is proposed that universities should actively seek *epistemic democracy* leading to universal participation of all students in terms of equality of all inquirers and 'knowers'. To illustrate what it means in practice, it may be useful to draw on an imaginary situation from Robert Dahl's book 'On Democracy' (2000), to clarify, in very basic terms, how universities and the TEF can support institutional epistemic justice. The book also offers a separate chapter on epistemic democracy.

In his book, Dahl (2000) describes a discussion among a group of people who know that they have to attain certain goals, but they cannot do it without working together. They therefore form an association based on the condition that all members are to be treated as though they were equally qualified to participate in the process of making decisions about the policies the association will pursue. The association therefore operates on the following agreed principles[1]:

Effective participation. Before a policy is adopted by the association, all members must have equal and effective opportunities for making their views known to other members about what the policy should be.

Voting equality. When the moment arrives at which the decision about policy will finally be made, every member must have an equal and effective opportunity to vote, and all votes must be counted as equal.

Enlightened understanding. Within reasonable limits as to time, each member must have equal and effective opportunities for learning about the relevant alternative policies and their likely consequences.

Control of the agenda. The members must have the exclusive opportunity to decide how and, if they choose, what matters are to be placed on the agenda. Thus the democratic process required by the three

---

[1]Please see full text Dahl, R. A. (2008). *On democracy.* Yale University Press, pp. 37–38.

preceding criteria is never closed. The policies of the association are always open to change by members, if they so choose.

Inclusion. All, or at any rate most, residents should have the full rights of citizens that are implied by the first four criteria.

The book highlights that there are good reasons for 'officially' adopting these particular criteria for a democratic process in the TEF, and other equivalent policies, as otherwise, as findings from literature on home and international students interactions tell us (see Chapter 2), international students, due to the lack of citizenship status in the country of education, colonial perceptions that they are inferior and consistent policy representations which position them as economic objects, are unlikely to be 'naturally' provided with opportunities for equal participation. Such inequalities are especially visible in Anglophone universities. It is therefore vitally important to create a space for criteria measuring democratic participation of international students in the TEF, to create a commonly agreed frame that will obligate universities to provide international students with opportunities for equivalence and to ensure that home students understand its benefits.

There are substantial gains arising from mobility of students, though they are not available to home learners who have been socialised by policy and political developments into thinking about international students as inferior. Home students, influenced by 'fear from foreign' and perceptions of their own superiority, lack willingness to engage with international students on politically and socially equal terms. They are however unable to change this on their own, and it is rarely their fault, as their lack of agency to do so is often restricted by limitations of their own social backgrounds and public discourses that question the value of studying alongside their international colleagues. Prof. Jane Callaghan has adequately captured such influences in her recent blog post[2] about the new Migration Advisory Committee survey, which was

---

[2]Please see for details the full blog—https://janeemcallaghan.wordpress.com/2018/05/16/home-office-it-is-not-ok-to-ask-our-students-about-the-impact-of-international-students-on-their-experience-of-university-life/.

commissioned to assess the impact of international students on home students' experiences of university: "In a multitude of ways the message is conveyed that the experience of the UK student is to be centred. How do 'They' affect you is the only question that matters. The International Student is considered of value only insofar as they positively impact UK students, and heaven help them if the hegemonically positioned British student suggests that the presence of foreigners in 'Their' universities troubles them".

So the public discourse never centres both groups as 'equals', but it is high time that it did! Brexit and higher education developments around the world make it more and more visible to international students that their experiences in the UK may not necessarily be based on conditions of reciprocal equality and democracy. Additionally, as more and more non-Anglophone countries enter the internationalisation competition (which is how internationalisation has come to be perceived, additionally contributing to experiences of subordination of international students), the book offers a form of caution to prevent the mistakes made in the UK. What are national policy and institutional rationales behind 'more energetic' recruitment of international students in non-Anglophone countries? How do these rationales compare to those in Anglophone countries? How, as a result, they may position and represent international students, and, most importantly, what consequences might they have for international students' realisation as democratic equals in the classroom? The book provides some answers to these questions in the chapters that follow.

Full answers to these questions are however difficult to formulate as literature on European perspectives regarding internationalisation has not yet fully explored issues of representations, and possible subordination of international students in European, non-Anglophone contexts. This book does not explore them either (although alludes to them throughout), but instead proposes a new idea—that there has to be a commitment to critical pedagogy, in the sense of Paulo Freire's emphasis on emancipation of the oppressed, which simultaneously leads to liberation of the oppressor (discussed in Chapter 4), that can be enacted through changes to official policies such as the TEF, AHELO or CALOHEE. We need to advocate for these changes this commitment now and create a standard policy framework for addressing questions of equity and democracy. We cannot risk waiting until there is more research about whether European policy representations of international students may or may not lead to their subordination. Then, it will be too late. Later in the book, I present emerging evidence suggesting that similarly to the UK, patterns of subordination of international students begin to emerge in Germany. This is worrying and should be seen as an alarm to act now. Prevention is always better than cure, and what we need now is a different set of metrics in policies attempting to assess teaching excellence in HE.

The book proposes these new metrics in Part III. Part III shows how some of the items from the UK Engagement Survey (UKES) can be used to encapsulate principles of epistemic inclusion of international students in the TEF. The proposed metrics can play a role in emancipating international students and liberating their home equivalents from the influence of public discourses that prevent the latter from seeing the gains that could be available to them through studying alongside their international colleagues. It is argued throughout the book that the current public discourses surrounding international students prevent their home peers from appreciating mutual and complimentary effects of assuming positions of 'subordinates' (in the sense of freeing themselves from the idea that home-grown knowledge is the 'right and only type of knowledge'). Adopting these positions is often needed, as otherwise, coloniality, understood in the book as a process that operates based on the logic of cultural, social and political domination over foreign students in an education system, can in fact create conditions for their own exclusion. Home students and universities need to understand this.

Expressions 'equal and effective opportunities' used by Dahl (2000) are especially significant for the metric proposed in Part III, as they are called upon in its design to draw attention to the teaching process that the proposed metric is hoped to encourage. 'Equal and effective opportunities' are encapsulated in the metric through the use of selected UKES items that aim to encourage just and free from coloniality pedagogies. These pedagogies are seen as *effective* when they create conditions for *equal participation*—meaning that the participation process, and those who co-coordinate it, need to actively invite contributions from people from all backgrounds, but without compromising the validity of people's own claims and views. Additional effectiveness of such a teaching process can therefore be manifested through the nature and scope of the understandings of teaching excellence the proposed metric can invite. These understandings are centred around ideas about evaluations of teaching quality through lenses of consistency in delivering transformation (what this means is explained in detail in Chapters 4 and 5). When such an understanding of teaching excellence is evoked through the TEF, evaluations of teaching are likely to be focused on process rather than benchmarked-based standards in higher education. So, what is then assessed is a type of pedagogical intentionality that is driven by equal, just and unprejudiced inclusion of all students in the classroom community. But such intentionality cannot be measured by any external indicators, nor could there be a cut-off point for it. The type of pedagogical intentionality described in the book is rather proposed to be assessed as consistency in delivering transformation that has no fixed 'target' or 'levels'—as inclusion and epistemic justice cannot be measured but such targets and levels. Rather, the aim is to show how each classroom performs to its own specifications, and this is explained in Chapters 6 and 7. It is generally argued in the book that only through inviting conceptualisations and understandings of teaching excellence that, inter alia, includes intellectual reciprocity with international students, the TEF can be reconceptualised from the state apparatus that supports socio-politically entrenched indoctrination that international students are inferior, to a vehicle that challenges this indoctrination and instead invites their democratic inclusion. In that sense, the TEF could be very powerful because, as explained in Chapter 1, as a national policy 'shaking up' university rankings, and therefore governance possibilities, it functions as a 'discursive practice' and a governance frame for many universities. It could therefore be a vehicle that delivers sustained liberation for both, international students (theorised as the oppressed in Chapter 4) and their home equivalents (who, using Freire's theorisations about critical pedagogy, could be described as oppressors).

There will be readers who will not like the idea of the proposed metric, either because they oppose metrics and rankings overall or because they will find some limitations of the model proposed in Chapters 6 and 7. In relation to the latter, these limitations certainly exit and they are mainly to do with the constraints of the UKES data. These limitations are discussed in Chapter 7. The introduction that follows after this preface additionally clarifies how the rankings in this book should not be understood. It needs to however be noted here that the main objective of designing the metrics proposed here and modelling selected UKES items was not to design a 'perfect' metric, but rather to conceptualise their design and show how they could work in practice (using any national data that has a similar focus to the UKES). The point of data modelling presented in Chapter 7 was to show that *it is* possible to design a metric that can provide information about *relationalities* between the characteristics of the teaching process and realisation of students as 'epistemic equals'. On the point of opposing rankings and metrics, whether we like it or not, in the current climate of commercialisation of higher education and the 'world class' university movement, rankings and metrics will not go away. It has been widely argued that rankings install homogenisation and drivers of policy and governance decisions because they embody common strategies. But this does not mean that we have no choice—we should instead fight fire with fire! This means designing a ranking that will (potentially globally!) create a standard framework for addressing questions of realisation of international students as equals and of freeing higher education teaching from coloniality. Such rankings could create an agreed frame, common to all universities, likely to trigger actions contributing to students' democratic life. There should be nothing wrong with homogenising universities in that sense.

Finally, it needs to be highlighted that the arguments in this book that emphasise the need for the new ranking to 'obligate' universities to be more inclusive *do not* intend to question the commitment of those who are truly concerned with just and democratic education. They have rather been formed to show that authentic inclusion of international students as 'equals' cannot be achieved through intercultural programs and curricular shifts carried out by individual persons. They are all extremely important, but the problem here is systemic and enabled by immigration and education policies, also including the TEF, which make universities colonised in mind and practice. The book therefore focuses on changing the system and has been written to deepen readers' consciousness about the fact that if we do not challenge the systemic hegemony that marginalises international students, our personal energies put towards realisation of international students as epistemic equals will go to waste.

xviii   Preface

The book is divided into three parts. Part I examines key theoretical ideas about 'policy a power'. It aims to show how through policies a hegemonic system of power relations is established and to highlight the fact that key issues affecting inclusion and equality of international students are mostly systemic. Part II looks in more detail at the influence of neo-liberalism and marketisation on the higher education system that marginalises international students and amplifies coloniality in education. Part II also begins to theorise the philosophical basis for a TEF ranking that could change this system. Part III offers a practical example of the systemic changes a new TEF ranking could achieve.

Keele, UK   Aneta Hayes

Contents

Part I Theorising Exclusion and Inequality Through Policy

1 Policy as Power   3

2 Policy Representations of International Students in the UK   29

**Part II Teaching Excellence in Higher Education
          and Internationalisation**

3 Conditionality as a Veiled Continuation of Coloniality
   vs. Epistemic Democracy   49

4 Pedagogy as a Political Act Towards Epistemic
   Democracy—The Type of Understanding of Teaching
   Excellence the TEF Can Shape?   75

5 Opportunities the TEF Can Offer   105

Part III A TEF Metric on Internationalisation and Epistemic Democracy—How Could it Work?

6 Suitable Data   131

7 Case Study   155

8 Concluding Remarks   177

Index   183

Abbreviations

AHELO	The Assessment of Higher Education Learning Outcomes
AUSSE	The Australasian Survey of Student Engagement
CAH2	The Level 2 of the Common Aggregation Hierarchy System, used by the Higher Education Statistics Agency (HESA) to classify subject disciplines in student degrees
CALOHEE	Measuring and Comparing Achievements of Learning Outcomes in Higher Education in Europe
CLA	The Collegiate Learning Assessment
HESA	The Higher Education Statistics Agency
ICC	The Intraclass Correlation Coefficient, explained in Chapter 6
NSS	The National Student Survey
NSSE	The National Survey of Student Engagement
TEF	The Teaching Excellence Framework
UKES	The UK Engagement Survey

List of Figures

Fig. 6.1	NSS questions constituting part of the TEF metrics—adapted from HEFCE consultation document—http://www.hefce.ac.uk/media/HEFCE,2014/Content/Pubs/2016/201632/HEFCE2016_32a-g.PDF	133
Fig. 6.2	Sample soft skills evaluated by UKES that may not be applicable to international students for reasons explained above, adapted from 2017 UKES Questionnaire	139
Fig. 7.1	Coding and labels for independent variables used in R	162
Fig. 7.2	Proposed subject groups for subject-level TEF based on the Level 2 of the Common Aggregation Hierarchy system—adapted from DfE (2018). Teaching Excellence and Student Outcomes Framework: subject-level: Consultation document, available from https://consult.education.gov.uk/higher-education-reform/teaching-excellence-and-student-outcomes-framework/	169
Fig. 7.3	Categories of courses and disciplines asked about in the UKES (Adapted from UKES Questionnaire 2017)	170

List of Tables

Table 4.1   CALOHEE framework for Civic, Social and Cultural Engagement (Adapted from CALOHEE Working Paper 2017, p. 7—https://www.calohee.eu/wp-content/uploads/2016/06/Working-Paper-for-Civic-Social-and-Cultural-Engagement.pdf)   87

Table 7.1   UKES questions proposed to be part of the design of the TEF metric on internationalisation and student predictors   160

Table 7.2   Estimates, standard errors, p-values (in parentheses) and predicted probabilities of feeling part of community   163

Table 7.3   Estimates, standard errors, p values (in parentheses) and predicted probabilities of feeing part of the community   164

Introduction

This introduction is a position chapter. It clarifies the contextual basis for some of the key arguments that are developed in the book. It also addresses some of the more contentious dimensions regarding the topics discussed, talks about the politics that may create resistance to the ideas outlined in the book and offers a preamble to how key points of the book *should not* be misunderstood.

As indicated in the preface, the two main goals of the book are (1) to consider changes to the TEF (and its international equivalents) that could re-construct the outdated representations of international students, presently contributing to their subordination in the classroom, and (2) to propose practical ways in which such changes could actually be implemented. These goals are located in theoretical frameworks of critical pedagogy and coloniality in education. The book positions that the changes to the TEF that are proposed can bring about sustained liberation from coloniality, for international and home students alike, as they are likely to prompt a type of classroom activism that can lead to epistemic democracy. It is argued in the book that coloniality, through operating broadly based on the logic of domination of home-grown perspectives and knowledge over foreign students in the education system,

xxvii

xxviii   **Introduction**

does not only prevent epistemic equivalence of international students but also limits home students' agency to access the benefits arising from internationalisation (something that will be described in the book as engendering violence in their oppressor). The book shows how coloniality is mostly enabled by policy representations of international students, which is why, it also argues that, by extension, coloniality can be challenged by adequate adjustments to policy.

Thus, the proposition in the book that the new shape of the TEF can offer sustained liberation *should not* be read as reflecting paternalism—in the sense that international students need to be liberated by others. Arguably, those who might think so have misunderstood Friere's work who does *not* propose that the oppressors need to be given greater authority and responsibility for freeing 'the others' from their oppression. It is appreciated here how the argument that metrics mandating home students and universities to engage with international students on more reciprocal terms could initially be seen as having that purpose. However, the deeper reading of the book should hopefully make it clear that this is *not* what is suggested at all. Instead, the proposition to include such metric in the TEF follows on from Friere's (1970) idea which advocates that the oppressed can be freed from their oppression if firstly, they themselves are active in fighting the oppression they face and secondly, if the oppressors are liberated from the forces that turn them into the oppressors. Liberation for the oppressors specifically can therefore happen mainly through opportunities and a desire to learn how they oppressed feel. Hence, the proposition in this book that reciprocity between the oppressor and the oppressed should underlie the new TEF metric. It is important to clarify however that 'measuring' this reciprocity through the TEF *does not* intend to put home students in charge of liberating the international students; this would reflect some of the aspects of conditionality and coloniality which this book critiques. Rather, it is proposed that this reciprocity is 'measured' to give home students opportunities to engage with identities of international students on equal terms, so they can ask questions about the different 'knowledges' that international students bring with them to the classroom and develop an understanding of how these 'knowledges' are subordinated if questions about them are not asked. Trough answering these questions, international students can simultaneously and actively participate in shaping this understanding, which will present them with opportunities to challenge their colonial oppression.

Friere (1970) posits that forces that turn individuals into oppressors are not a given destiny but are rather the result of an unjust order that engenders violence in the oppressors. The proposition of changing the TEF with metrics on internationalisation follows on from this idea, deconstructing in the first instance the role of public policy discourses in engendering intellectual and epistemic violence towards international students, and consequently arguing that this violence can be changed if policy constructions of international students are changed. Critical policy studies reviewed in the book suggest that public policy representations of international students that challenge their intellectual value have given some legitimacy to home students' thinking that it is okay to be superior towards their international colleagues. The book is therefore suggesting that this kind of thinking can also be 'un-legitimised' through relevant policy changes, based on a simple logic that—as there are ways in which it is possible to see how policies had shaped intellectual superiority over international students, they can also, if adequately changed, encourage more equivalence of alternative 'knowledges'.

However, what is *not* suggested by the book is that there is a need to create metrics that draw attention to equivalence of knowledge produced by international students because those students cannot make their own voices to be heard. The discussion in Chapter 2 about international students as 'objects', positioned as such by public, policies, should therefore *not* be read as a suggestion that international students are unable to effect any change for themselves. Whilst the book contains a critique of structural power, concluding that opportunities for international students of being included as epistemic equals are limited (at the very least!) by policy constructions, it is by no means implied that international students do not have any transformative potential. They of course have their own agency, the book does not dispute this. The main purpose of this critique, however, is to draw attention to the fact that the power of international students' agency and the process of self-formation of international students in the higher education system of the host country always takes place 'within conditions of disequilibrium

xxx   Introduction

in which student subjects manage their lives reflexively, fashioning their own changing identities, albeit under social circumstances largely beyond their control' (Marginson 2014, p. 6). What the book therefore aims to achieve, through proposing to change the structural power, is an official acknowledgment of the status of international students as epistemic equals, which will arguably give them greater control over those structural circumstances which presently prevent social change at universities that could lead to acceptance of foreigners in the education system as equals. If the current disequilibrium in which international students have to negotiate their identities is caused by structural factors, again, the simple logic would suggest that the effects of this disequilibrium can be reversed via adequate structural changes.

Naturally, international students are likely to have some 'allies' outside of policy. These allies usually come into international students' lives via individual friendships or, for instance, university tutors who, through individual efforts and curricular changes in their programmes, work towards greater inclusion of international students. The presence of these 'allies' can in itself create possibilities for transformations and indeed, it may even directly or indirectly influence relationships with international students at the level of individual institutions (e.g. Spiro 2014). But what the book additionally asks is whether tutors improve relationships with international students to do the bidding of the powerful? In their mind, intentionally or not, their efforts to 'help out' international students may still be driven by conditional equality (this is discussed in detail in Chapter 3). What is therefore required is a change in the socio-political consciousness that presently might be encouraging such conditional equality. This can happen if policy is changed because, as the book will argue, policy shapes such consciousness through its role as 'exteriority' that can enable new things to be said about international students. This is explained later on in the book by quoting Foucault (2002) who argues that objects themselves cannot enable new things to be said about them, rather, they need some kind of exteriority that has the power of enabling these things to be said and for a new reality to come into being. And whilst Foucault was not an advocate of transformation through policy, it is argued here, through the review of policy as 'discursive practice' in Chapter 1 and policy representations of international students in Chapter 2, that policy can be exactly the type of exteriority that international students may need to be included as epistemic equals. This latter argument is supported by discussions in the book which show that policy functions as a master process of othering or accepting individuals in an education system.

The change in nationally perpetuated representations of international students from 'objects' to 'equal knowers' can however be difficult when there is no backing from policy. It will be explained in Chapter 1 that what is said in policy is also said by people affected by it and reflected in their actions (e.g. Howarth 2010). By extension, and if adequately changed, policy can therefore create relevant political backing for a change in positioning of international students because, through being the headway for creating new ways of talking about things and people, it can lead to a change in political consciousness about who international students are. Unfortunately, the review of literature in this book on the topic of integration of international students as epistemic equals reveals limits of universities' commitment to ending epistemic violence. This literature shows that universities, at the level of policy, advocate practising epistemic justice but as long as it does not disturb the existing socio-political order and as long as it does not challenge the epistemic privilege of the host country. Through this, policies in the host country therefore 'excuse' universities from any social-political change as these policies do not insist on problematising epistemic justice as an integral part of university development. They enable through this 'official thinking', and in some instances even insist, that home perspectives should remain normative.

Of course, it is not assumed in the book that once the proposed metrics become part of the TEF, change in the actual engagement with international students will automatically happen. It could be argued though that the official constructions of international students are more likely to change as when policy represents international students as equally qualified knowers, these ideas will enter the public discourse, and through that, international students are more likely to be officially accepted as such. A changed discourse surrounding international students may however still not be sufficient to ensure their inclusion as epistemic equals because, as we learn, for instance, from the Australian

xxxii Introduction

research, official discourses and narratives about an issue do not always translate into practice (Marginson 2012). The findings from the Australian context have shown that despite being acknowledged as having equal human rights by the Universal Declaration of Human Rights, international students' de jure rights often did not translate to de facto rights. The power of this universal policy in protecting international students from discrimination was seen in the research to be limited by other intervening and mediating factors that affected the reception of international students, as well as enabled universal human rights to be manipulated locally in the country of education (Marginson 2012). Some of these mediating factors in the Australian case were political, which is why it is argued here that the current politics surrounding internationalisation and international students' representations are likely to play a significant role in building resistance to the TEF changes this book proposes. To understand how the politics surrounding internationalisation might affect these changes, it will be important for readers to consider the arguments outlined in the book about the context of increasingly marketised attitudes towards internationalisation and its structural referents, which are shaped by commercial university ranking. These arguments are presented throughout the book and surface the idea that reputational and financial gains that come with good 'performance' in the internationalisation category do not require more critical relationships with international students which, in turn, affect any developments in terms of epistemic democracy.

Perhaps that is why 'problems' such as lack of engagement of academics and little attention to the professional development of academic and administrative staff with regards to internationalisation (Hunter et al. 2018) still exist. Engaging academics and admin staff in internationalisation would however require an official public strategy to fight coloniality. This could however be difficult, as it would, in the first place, require acknowledging that coloniality exists. The problem however is that admitting that coloniality exists is very political and it would require a complete ideological change. Presently, however, due to the structural referents of internationalisation, which give significant ratings to measures related to internationally co-authored papers and international-home students and staff ratios, such a change is not required and universities can 'get away' with not doing much in terms of epistemic democracy, whilst still be seen as highly internationalised. Consequently, investment in the progress academic and administrative staff could make in terms of epistemic democracy is likely to be left in the background. Hunter et al. (2018) posit this could be changed through adequate training as 'facilitated intervention may help academics and administrative staff who lack international and intercultural experience to explore what internationalisation means in their discipline and how to deliver it through the curriculum [and relevant pedagogies—my emphasis]. The book agrees but additionally argues that we first need to tackle the problem of the invisibility of the issue that academics do not feel it is their responsibility to change coloniality. For this issue to become visible, it needs to be acknowledged in policy and in official referents of internationalisation—otherwise, the politics connected with balancing the level of benefit that commercialisation of internationalisation brings to universities vs. zero benefits (at least in the commercial sense!) arising from eradicating dehumanisation of international students could get in the way.

Having an official strategy to fight coloniality could of course create a further political problem, which is to do with the notion that universities remain nationally and locally rooted. The book *is not* suggesting that the national connection of universities purposely dehumanises international students, but rather that the sense of national pride and the frequent emphasis on locally produced knowledge, as well as the notion that universities should mainly operate for the common good of nationals, may cause a political tension with regards to epistemic democracy. There might be various aspects with regards to which this political tension may develop. For example, one such tension is related to nationally unchallenged ideas of what constitutes valid knowledge, despite diversity and the intellectual contribution of international 'knowledges' being officially promoted within a nation state (Tannock 2018). Another political aspect may be related to questions about what happens to the international knowledge during and after the official enrolment of international students in host country institutions (ibid). What is the relative position of this knowledge when home and international students study together and what is its position after international

xxxiv Introduction

students leave the host country institutions? In countries like Britain, it seems that there is not much desire to make use of this knowledge as, for instance, international students are immediately urged to leave the country before they even have a chance to implement it the British labour market. The politicians there argue that visa controls that make international students leave immediately after the completion of their studies are necessary 'to put the interests of the British people first' (Morgan 2016, p. i).

In continental Europe, a similar protectionist perspective is perhaps most pronounced in the Netherlands, when the political and social tensions surrounding courses taught in English have clearly started to emerge. Universities throughout Europe, as well as elsewhere in the world, have been increasingly moving towards teaching in English, to attract more international students. In the Netherlands, where 74% of Masters and 23% of Bachelor degree programmes are now taught in English (Salomone 2018), the tensions surrounding this situation have probably been greater than elsewhere. In 2015, Beter Onderwijs Nederland (Better Education Netherlands), popularly known as BON, issued a manifesto and an official call for action against the move towards more courses in English. It had been felt that large numbers of international students flocking the country affected the accessibility and quality of higher education offered to Dutch students and the loss of the Dutch language as a vehicle for intellectual engagement and knowledge production (Salomone 2018). BON also felt that the move towards teaching in English was actually against the law adopted in 1991 via Article 7.2 of the Higher Education Law which states that:

> teaching and examinations must be conducted in Dutch except if the training is related to another language or in the context of a lecture given by a foreign teacher, or if the specific nature, organisation or quality of teaching or the nationality of the students so requires, according to a code of conduct adopted by the university's executive board (cited in Salomone 2018, p. ii).

Consequently, in May 2018, the Association of Universities in the Netherlands (VSNU) issued a joint paper agreeing to place an upper limit on courses in English, in order to control the numbers of international students arriving in the Netherlands and thereby to *protect* the quality and accessibility of education for Dutch students (Salomone 2018). This seems to resonate with the rationale Amber Rudd, former Home Secretary, put forward when justifying greater visa control for students arriving in the UK, which was driven by undercurrents of *protecting* 'the interests of the British people first' (Morgan 2016, p. i).

It is therefore possible to see how international students' rights to knowledge production can easily be affected by such political developments. The idea of a university being mostly for the nationals and the emphasis on nationally produced knowledge being given political legitimacy create conditions for epistemological privilege of home grown perspectives, which consequently become constitutive of coloniality. Coloniality is discussed in more detail in Part II of the book, but it is important to note here that the very existence of such epistemological privilege creates an education system which legitimises certain forms of knowledge and silences others. Part II also highlights how the current trends to recruit more international students bring a deep tension between the said form of educational nationalism and epistemic democracy. These tensions are mentioned here to draw attention to the fact that the changes to the TEF prosed in this book, which essentially include a proposition to create metrics that place international students' knowledge on par with that produced at home, are likely to trigger political and social responses that may affect the possibility of these changes ever being implemented.

For example, some of the responses to my earlier work on which this book builds, have already questioned my critique of the political reasons behind silencing international students in the classroom, positing that it is legitimate to expect international students to accept the host country perspective on education. One particular reviewer argued that it is acceptable that international students are responsible to adapt to the system, teaching approaches and knowledge taught in the host country university. But while this is pragmatically required, because international students still need to pass the exams and meet the requirements of their degree classification, it should not be done with the view to conditioning international students towards inclusion and therefore enabling host country universities to work on the assumption that their teaching can remain unchanged. Fighting coloniality through classroom activism that is hoped to be triggered by the changes to the TEF rankings proposed in this book represents a critical response to such comments; these changes are hoped to lead to a social change that will eventually reflect a sustained political, social and educational acknowledgement that home perspectives are poorer, in value and content, if they are not critiqued through the lenses of knowledge produced outside the realms of the nation state.

However, so long as the current level of politics surrounding internationalisation is maintained, such an acknowledgment is unlikely to take place. That is precisely why the book sets to target the levels of politicisation of internationalisation, not through individual contestation of and discrete resistance to discrimination of international students are facing (which are of course valuable and needed), but rather through the meta-frameworks of policy which, despite creating the current levels of politics surrounding internationalisation in the first place, can also represent a more collective voice calling for change. Through proposing that reciprocity with international perspectives should be an official ranking related to teaching, the book uses the polity's own weapon, to fight fire with fire. This in itself is political and should therefore *not* be taken to mean that the book proposes that the TEF can be depoliticised. By its very virtue of being a national ranking, the TEF will always be political, so will any changes that are made to it. But it is at the same time argued that because of the nature and scope of the proposed changes, which emphasise how universities independently of their peer institutions and according to their own specifications work towards epistemic democracy, the TEF can make internationalisation less political.

It is argued in the book that there is something very apolitical about proposing to measure the outcomes that are discussed in Part III. These outcomes are theorised in Chapter 4 and it is additionally demonstrated how they could be measured in practice in Chapters 6 and 7. Chapter 5 references several critiques of the TEF but none of these critiques have so far focused on the opportunities for depoliticisation of internationalisation the exercise can bring about. These opportunities are about making an ideological shift in terms of what national rankings actually measure and through that, how they can depoliticise internationalisation by turning a university desire to internationalise into a question about, and a referent of, critical pedagogy and epistemic democracy.

It is true that pedagogy can also be politicised, of course, especially when it comes to multiculturalism and inclusion (e.g. McLaren 1995; Giroux 2018). But if the relationality between inclusion and the teaching process within each individual university is set to be one of the main outcomes that is measured in national rankings related to teaching, without any set standards or cut-off points indicating beforehand of what it should be, then the political influence on internationalisation is likely to be reduced. Universities would still be assessed; they would have to demonstrate how they work towards pedagogical intentionality that is inclusive of all students as equals, but this assessment would not be hierarchical. Rather, it would be based on referents that show how each university performs according to their own specification.

Additionally, the proposed changes to the TEF could make internationalisation even less political because they would 'measure' it as an internal process, based on the proviso that epistemic democracy is a referent of internationalisation that is constantly evolving (Knight 2004). It is on this basis that it is argued in the book that measures of internationalisation can be less political because if applied in ways that are outlined in Chapters 6 and 7, they could be detached from any national goals and self-interests that shape the current (mis-) understandings of internationalisation (De Wit 2015; Knight 2014). These misunderstandings include ideas that internationalisation, for instance, means teaching in the English language, that it reflects a desire to increase student mobility, or strives to include more internationally focused curricula and is driven by increased recruitment of international students (ibid). Whilst all these are institutional strategies connected with internationalisation, achieving these should not be mistaken for the process of internationalisation as such, as this process has no end goals (Knight 2004). However, as shown in this book, the influence of commercial rankings has shaped understandings of internationalisation that is contrary to its conceptualisation as a continually evolving process, representing it instead as a linear strategy built on 'inputs and outputs', with pragmatic institutional goals leading to specific ends. These ends have been politicised through their use in national and international rankings and as a means to building institutional prestige. On the contrary, it is argued that the metrics proposed in this book can re-articulate the meaning of internationalisation back to its understandings as a process of integration that is constantly evolving, and it is hoped that through assessing it as such, they have the potential to make the whole process less political.

Arguably, the creators of the TEF are not likely to warm to the idea of moving away from benchmarks and absolute measures. Responses and critiques challenging the possibility of ever 'measuring' anything for comparability, especially without the use of benchmarks, are likely to emerge. But trying to use benchmarks to measure such outcomes would of course be an impossible situation to square. Recent reports on a study that looked into measuring 'learning gain' through the TEF concluded that capturing learning gain would be impossible as a metric in the TEF because such measures are too context-specific (McKie 2018). This book however argues otherwise, and shows in Chapter 7, a statistical model that could enable comparability measurements that are relative and that take into account a number of contextual factors related to both, teaching and students' individual characteristics.

Critiques of the proposed model are however likely to follow. Drawing on the previous critiques that have emerged in response to the current shape and design of the TEF, it is likely that someone commentators will critique the potential level of the administrative burden for institutions the use of the proposed statistical model may be seen to cause. The book is particularly critical of such potential responses, given the already heavy administrative burden the proposals for the subject-level TEF are going to impose on institutions. For instance, the newest government plans for the subject-level TEF will require institutions to make up to thirty-six subject-level submissions (based on the discipline classification system, the Common Aggregation Hierarchy (CAH) that will be used in the TEF to classify subject disciplines), plus an institutional subject submission (DfE 2018). Additionally, as recently analysed by Wonkhe (an independent higher education forum), first reports of the subject-level TEF in 2021 will contain old data as most of them will refer to cohorts and institutional information from years that have already happened (Kernohan 2018). Thus, 'the spread of cohorts whose experience will be considered in subject TEF is now a vast 8 years, covering students who graduated between 2011 and 2019. Even with the minimum proposed distance between awards (four years), 2025 could see institutions making claims about the student experience and outcomes of the class of 2008' (Kernohan 2018, p. i). The model for the metrics proposed in this book, on the other hand, always takes account of the current data, producing measures that focus on how institutions perform in a given year and according to their own specifications. The model focuses on measuring relationalities between the characteristics of the teaching process and realisation of students as epistemic equals, taking account of any changing characteristics of the students and the teaching on their courses. All this is captured by the reports from one set of data, collected by the sector year on year, which is a representation that is unlike any other of the current TEF metrics (as these currently contain aggregated information from a number of surveys and outdated national data sets). It should therefore not be difficult to see how the current aspects of the TEF, rather than the model that is proposed in this book, that create an administrative burden for institutions.

The main undercurrent of the proposed metric is that the relationality it measures cannot be considered in any absolute terms (i.e. measured through benchmarks) because relationality in itself it is a relative concept. There are therefore no absolutes against which the outputs from 'measuring' this relationality can be benchmarked. Instead, the statistical model presented in Chapter 7 shows that intra- and inter-institutional comparisons are still possible without the use of any such benchmarks. The biggest *practical* contribution of this book therefore lies in conceptualising how these comparisons can be implemented through the TEF and operationalising them through sample data modelling presented in Part III of the book.

Furthermore, some critiques may also raise concerns about the degree to which any rankings can in fact be liberatory, especially in the sense that is proposed in the book—that is, to what extent they can facilitate liberation from academic silencing. As noted recently by Loukkola

xl   Introduction

(2018, p. i), 'every year, there are more rankings and more different types of focus, but rankings are inherently able to tell only one part of a much wider story'. Rankings continue to assess universities mostly on research criteria, leaving educational or societal missions behind. Only recently, rankings started to include referents related to teaching, but these referents do not yet target changes to the institutions' societal contexts that could facilitate liberation from epistemic oppression. Instead, academic literature argues that even the newer rankings that have emerged in recent years continue to 'privilege and valorise knowledge systems that derive from historically epistemically privileged positions (i.e. Global North)' (Shahjahan et al. 2017, p. 68). These rankings operate under epistemological dimensions that have been shaped by histories of universities and their prestige, consequently affecting international relations in the education system and leading to violence manifested in discrimination of certain types of knowledge (ibid). Thus, this book aims to propose rankings that emphasise academic subjectivities of all people and that valorise ways in which all people are encouraged to contribute them in the classroom. The statistical model discussed in Chapters 6 and 7 encourages universities to start creating knowledge production systems that are not conceptually trapped in the nation states and their connection to universities. Rather, the model highlights how epistemic silencing accomplished by the current referents in commercial rankings can be ended and proposes that the main assessment outcome in these rankings should be the process through which universities commit to ending it.

Finally, the new rankings proposed in this book *should not* be seen as offering a somewhat narrow approach to solving the problem of epistemic democracy, which, as indicated above is a deeply complex political and historical problem. For instance, if we change what happens within UK universities, through the proposed TEF metrics, but do not transform the fact that UK universities are still seen as aspirational locations of study for both UK students and international students alike, how much are the proposed TEF changes going to be able to shift the unequal and colonial global power inequalities that prioritise the elite global status of UK universities? Some concerns with regards to the point about the prestige of Anglophone knowledge are raised

Introduction **xli**

in Chapter 2, where examples from research in Germany are cited, showing that the discrimination the students in the study were facing, despite taking place within the borders of Germany, was largely based on the fact that some international students did not match the characteristics of students from the Anglophone countries. In light of such findings, what would be fair to say about the rakings proposed here, basing it precisely on the fact that the proposed rankings could have influence also beyond the context of the UK (if they were considered in assessments such as AHELO, CALOHEE or the CLA), is that their implementation should at least mobilise some thinking in higher education about 'pluralis[ing] the future by pluralising knowledge in the present (…) to produce more honest and wider range of options—material, ideational and normative—for human beings and societies to choose from' (Nandy 2000, p. 122). Arguably, this could shift some thinking about the need to prioritise access to and knowledge production by Anglophone universities as the new type of rankings proposed in this book would help advance the view that development takes place not through falling in step with Anglophone knowledge, but rather through discussions in the classroom that are situated within epistemological and ontological traditions of all people who attend them. Given the findings from the German case specially, the book proposes to extend the changes to the TEF to its sister assessment exercises around the world (AHELO, CALOHEE and the CLA), so universities across the globe start creating knowledge production systems according to the epistemological specifications of their own classrooms, and *not* in relation to those shaped by the Anglophone elites.

Thus, it is argued that, if introduced into the TEF and/or its sister equivalents, the proposed rankings could 'measure' university aspirations for epistemic inclusion that are not based on conditionality. It is plausible to think that based on these rankings universities could start working towards greater equivalence of all 'knowledges', because they would be assessed on their commitment to ending epistemic silencing. The next chapter reviews key theorisations about policy and rankings as power, to strengthen this point and to show how 'things' that policy frames as important or problematic are consequently deemed as such.

xlii Introduction

Frankly speaking, this is exactly what the book aims to achieve—an official acknowledgement that epistemic inequality is a problem in our universities, because only when it is acknowledged as such, and when new rankings 'measure' how universities work towards eradicating it, it is more likely to be dealt with.

References

De Wit, H. (2015). Internationalization misconceptions. *International Higher Education, 64*, 1–6. https://ejournals.bc.edu/ojs/index.php/ihe/article/view/8556/8321.

Department for Education (DfE). (2018). *Teaching excellence and student outcomes framework: Subject level government consultation response.* Accessed on 15 November 2018. Retrieved from https://assets.publishing.service.gov.uk/government/uploads/system/uploads/attachment_data/file/750411/TEF_government_response.pdf.

Foucault, M. (2002). *Archaeology of knowledge.* Abingdon: Routledge.

Freire, P. (1970). *Pedagogy of the oppressed.* New York: Continuum (published as Penguin Classics 2017).

Giroux, H. (2018). *Pedagogy and the politics of hope: Theory, culture, and schooling: A critical reader.* London: Routledge.

Howarth, D. (2010). Power, discourse, and policy: Articulating a hegemony approach to critical policy studies. *Critical Policy Studies, 3*(3–4), 309–335.

Hunter, F., Jones, E., & de Wit, H. (2018, November 2). *The staff who are overlooked in internationalisation.* Accessed on 12 November 2018. Retrieved from http://www.universityworldnews.com/article.php?story=20181031081234166.

Kernohan, D. (2018, October 22). Policy watch: Subject TEF year 2. *Wonkhe.* Accessed on 8 November 2018. Retrieved from https://wonkhe.com/blogs/policy-watch-subject-tef-year-2/.

Knight, J. (2004). Internationalization remodeled: Definition, approaches, and rationales. *Journal of Studies in International Education, 8*(1), 5–31.

Knight, J. (2014). Is internationalisation of higher education having an identity crisis? In A. Maldonado-Maldonado & R. M. Bassett (Eds.), *The forefront of international higher education* (pp. 75–87). Dordrecht: Springer.

Loukkola, T. (2018, November 9). The making of university rankings—Has anything changed? *University World News.* Accessed on 12 November

2018. Retrieved from http://www.universityworldnews.com/article.php?story=20181108091550772.

Marginson, S. (2012). Including the other: Regulation of the human rights of mobile students in a nation-bound world. *Higher Education, 63*(4), 497–512.

Marginson, S. (2014). Student self-formation in international education. *Journal of Studies in International Education, 18*(1), 6–22.

McLaren, P. (1995). *Critical pedagogy and predatory culture: Oppositional politics in a postmodern era.* London: Routledge.

McKie, A. (2018). Learning gain metrics 'cannot be used to compare universities'. *Times Higher Education.* Accessed on 1 Mar 2019. Available from https://www.timeshighereducation.com/news/learning-gain-metricscannot-be-used-compare-universities.

Morgan, J. (2016). UK government to toughen student visa rules for 'low quality' courses. *Times Higher Education.* Accessed on 10 November 2018. Retrieved from https://www.timeshighereducation.com/news/uk-government-toughen-student-visa-rules-low-quality-courses.

Nandy, A. (2000). Recovery of indigenous knowledge and dissenting futures of the university. In S. Inayatullah & J. Gidely (Eds.), *The university in transformation: Global perspectives and the future of the university*, (pp. 115–123). Westport, CT: Bergin & Garvey.

Salomone, R. (2018, July 27). Dutch court defers decision on English in universities. *University World News.* Accessed on 06 November 2018. Retrieved from http://www.universityworldnews.com/article.php?story=20180724140627526.

Shahjahan, R. A., Blanco Ramirez, G., & Andreotti, V. D. O. (2017). Attempting to imagine the unimaginable: A decolonial reading of global university rankings. *Comparative Education Review, 61*(S1), S51–S73.

Spiro, J. (2014). Learning interconnectedness: Internationalisation through engagement with one another. *Higher Education Quarterly, 68*(1), 65–84.

Tannock, S. (2018). *Educational equality and international students.* London: Springer.

Part I

Theorising Exclusion and Inequality Through Policy

1

Policy as Power

This opening chapter of the book examines key theoretical ideas about 'policy as power' and as 'discursive practice'. It aims to show how, through policies, a hegemonic system of power relations can be established and to highlight the fact that key issues affecting inclusion and equality of international students are mostly systemic. To support this argument, the chapter cites research evidence which shows that even in situations when attempts to create an alternative 'discursive practice' are made by international students, these attempts still engender actions, interpretations and subjectivities of students that feed, rather than challenge, the hegemonic system of policy and regulatory frameworks that 'determine' international students' lives in the country of education. By extension, drawing on the same theoretical ideas, the chapter also posits that epistemic democratisation of university classrooms based on inclusion of international students' knowledges as equals will only start when it is 'recommended' by policies and officially 'measured' through university rankings. The chapter begins to highlight the potential contribution of the TEF in this area.

Policy is power. Through policies, various stakeholder intentions are realised, which reflect planned rationality to, for instance, reinforce the

© The Author(s) 2019
A. Hayes, *Inclusion, Epistemic Democracy and International Students*,
https://doi.org/10.1007/978-3-030-11401-5_1

status quo, when things are going well (or when it is politically conven- ient to keep them as they are), or to legitimate new authority, when a specific need for change has been identified. Policy making therefore cannot be separated from politics, as public policies always reflect the view of the state on a particular issue and in that sense, are a vehicle for accomplishment of specific goals which are related to this view. Thus, policies set agendas, generate ways forward and lay out guidelines for adoption of particular proposals. Through such roles, they function as power and become a framework for acting and governing. These func- tions of policies have been theorised by Foucault (1969, printed in English in 2002) and more contemporary analysts of his work (e.g. Bacchi and Bonham 2014) as 'discursive practice', mainly intending to denote an effect of policies on producing specific types of knowledge (discourse) and the work they do (practice). This understanding of 'dis- cursive practice', whether developed directly via Foucault's theorisations or not, have been used in policy studies to shape our understanding of distributive impacts of policy on organisations and individuals, ration- ales underlying them and consequences for creating educational ine- qualities (e.g. Fischer 2003; Taylor 2004; Zembylas 2005; Ball 2012; Thomson et al. 2013). In short, policies functioning as 'discursive prac- tices' set the 'truth' and then shape our responses to that 'truth', because they permit some actions, prohibit others, and most importantly for the arguments developed later on in the chapter, rationalise new ones. Foucault (2002) explains such policy effects in the following way:

> The conditions necessary for the appearance of an object of discourse [here international students], the historical conditions required if one is to 'say anything' about it, and if several people are to say different things about it, the conditions necessary if it is to exist in relation to other objects, if it is to establish with them relations of resemblance, proximity, difference, distance, transformation, (…) these conditions are many and imposing. Which means that one cannot speak of anything at any time. It is not easy to say something new, it is not enough for us to open our eyes and to pay attention, or to be aware, for new objects to suddenly to light up and emerge from the ground. But this difficulty is not only a negative one, it must not be attached to some obstacle whose power appears to

1 Policy as Power 5

be, exclusively, to blind, to hinder, to prevent discovery (...) the object [still] exists under the positive conditions of a complex group of relations. These relations are established between institutions, economic and social processes, behavioural patters, systems of norms, types of classification and modes of characterisation that are not present in the object (...) [but rather] in the field of exteriority. (Foucault 2002, pp. 49–50)

Such theorisations would therefore seem to suggest that in order for us to 'say something new' about international students, something that could act as an effective 'counterweight' to the current policy representations of international students that legitimate their subordination (explained in Chapter 2), there has to be a new 'exteriority', in the form of a fresh policy discourse. Such discourse could then create avenues for saying new things about international students and, as already alluded to in the introduction, for opening home students' eyes to the intellectual benefits international mobility can offer to them. As explained by Foucault (2002), objects themselves cannot enable new things to be said about them, rather, it is policy (as exteriority) that has the power of enabling these things to be said and for a new reality to come into being. It is in those terms that policy functions as discursive practice, which is contingent on the sense-making of 'influential' individuals who can drive decisions to create possibilities for a new status, social and educational privileges and representations of 'others' in society (e.g. Foucault 2002). Functioning as discursive practice, policies can therefore dictate behaviours that 'install new regimes of truth' (Bacchi and Bonham 2014, p. 177). That is why they are called 'discursive practice' and not merely a 'discourse' because their meaning encloses whole systems of thought, guidance for this thought and subsequent actions, which permit what consequently happens in real life (Bacchi and Bonham 2014).

The history surrounding the things that are said about an object is also important (Foucault 2002). That is why rationales behind internationalisation in Britain are reviewed through historical and sociopolitical lenses in Chapter 2. This review highlights that ways in which policies act as power are not merely a matter of saying something about somebody else, but are rather linked to the total package that includes not only what is said but also how what is said is justified to be 'true'

6   A. Hayes

and which political, historical and social aspects of the context can be drawn upon to understand why it is justified in this way. As argued by Young (1987, cited in Bacchi and Bonham 2014, p. 178), understanding discursive practice is

> not simply that which was thought or said per se, but all the discursive rules and categories that were a priori, assumed as a constituent part of discourse and therefore of knowledge. (Young 1987, p. 48)

Chapter 2 unravels key political and historical parts of the discourse surrounding international students, to reveal how knowledge about them in the British society has come about. These parts are also critiqued to understand the basis on which it was possible to say certain 'things' about international students—that is, how things said could be in the 'true' (Foucault 2002). This book therefore provides important understandings of what kind of social and especially educational 'lives' the knowledge about international students has created for them and how policy has functioned over the years as the dominant power in the creation of these lives.

To understand the role of policy in creating lives for people, it is important to position 'policy' itself as a subject of study and exploration. The nature and scope of things that are said about individuals in policies has an undeniable socio-cultural dimension which, as already alluded to above, reflects a government's 'take' on an issue. That is why the nature and scope of these things need to be explored. Questions about its sources and rationales need to be asked, to understand not only how specific representations of, for instance, international students have come about, but also what implications these representations might have for their participation and inclusion in the country of education. This simultaneously means trying to understand the government's thinking behind ways in which they believe order should be maintained and how specific 'types' of individuals, such as international students, will presumably 'live within and abide by the rules' that are produced in policies to set this order (Bacchi 2009, p. ix). Bacchi (2009) argues that developing this understanding could be done through an approach to policy analysis that focuses on unpicking 'What's the problem represented to be?'

(WPR). This approach is used throughout the book for two reasons: firstly, to help bring to bear understandings of ways in which policies related to internationalisation have so far 'determined' the lives of international students in the UK, and secondly, and by extension, to support some of the key arguments that are made in the book about the need for new policies, such as the TEF, to include specific metrics on internationalisation that can bring about changes in these lives.

The WPR approach is discussed in more detail a bit later in this chapter. But here it is worth citing some research findings which suggest that even in situations whereby international students establish for themselves alternative ways of being, for example, through some emotional responses to the reality created for them by regulatory frameworks of policies, these alternative ways are not strong enough to 'combat' the disadvantaging effects of policies. Such findings further support the notion that policy is power.

I have argued elsewhere that subjectivities of student interpretations of their situation in the country of education, while making international students 'feel better' on a personal level, can never counter-act the powerful master processes of discrimination organised for them through policies (Hayes 2018). The data I had collected as part of the research on the types of discrimination international students were experiencing in the country of education have shown that, whilst students were able to create positive emotions for themselves when they, for instance, experienced racism, and that these emotions helped them to cope with the effects of abuse they were experiencing, they at the same time became an additional function of discriminatory forces originally instituted by legal and structural dimensions of the social and educational domains in which the students were interacting. The emotions that were present in the students who took part in the research, such as self-comforting that the abuse they were experiencing was soon going to be over as their studies were coming to an end, indeed became another 'type' of discursive practice. This type of discursive practice however further fed into the reality already established by policies, as the emotions that were evoked in the students did not prompt them to take any action against the discrimination they were experiencing. Instead, the students were subsumed by these emotions into accepting discrimination and engendered actions, performances and interpretations that further marginalised their already marginalised status in the country of education.

The sample excerpts from international students that are cited below show ways in which the students in the research established a new reality for themselves through some unspoken interpretations of the microaggressions they were experiencing. These interpretations were evoked when they were struggling for acceptance and access to the same social and educational benefits as the home students, and when they were looking for ways to manage the sense of self through creating self-imaginaries of self and who they were for the country of education. Importantly, these self-imaginaries were different from the understandings of who the international students were for the country of education which had been shaped by official international policies. But even more importantly, they were not sufficient to contraindicate the negative effects of the latter, as it is the latter that had 'power' of deciding who they were, through being attached to the system that was difficult to challenge by personal 'coping strategies'.

Thus, a common strategy among international students, for instance, was to remain 'invisible', even if that meant being perceived as academically unsuccessful. This fed the existing perceptions of international students as 'inferior', created to a large extent by national policies and public discourses which, traditionally, have shaped views that differing learning behaviours of international students need to be corrected to study in the prestigious British education system (Hayes 2018). The student cited below was aware of these views, but instead of trying to challenge them, they adopted strategies that, on the one hand created a feeling of internal satisfaction and security, but on the other, simultaneously reinforced the common perceptions of international students as people who are in educational deficit. The student was aware of these complimentary effects of their decision to remain 'invisible', but their emotional well-being was more important for them. In that sense, the 'compromise' that the student had made became a new 'discursive practice' for them. It did not however work in opposition to the damaging effects of international students' representations in policies. It rather worked in tandem with these representations, creating additional conditions for their exclusion.

> Interviewer: Did you ever feel you were unsuccessful, you know, if you think about your engagement here, academically?

1 Policy as Power   9

Student: Inside I do feel I'm successful but from outside I think that like, these instructors think that I am unsuccessful because I didn't participate in the class discussions. I mean because of like the, I don't want to make the other British people looking at me like 'What are you talking about, I can't understand you'. I don't want them to think like that, that's why I always prefer to remain silent in the classes.

Interviewer: And so you say that inside you felt successful but you don't think that other people perceived you as successful because of that?

Student: Yes.

Interviewer: Okay. Student:... because I don't want to be evaluated by my non-nativeness, I mean, I don't want to be...I don't want, that's the point, I just want to be equal with the other native students. (TESOL student, University B)

The quotes that follow additionally encapsulate a series of ways in which the emotional impact of student self-interpretations of the discrimination they were experiencing, which again seemed to function as some sort of 'discursive practices', also ran in a range of social contexts. For example, aware of their ethnic, cultural and race differences, some students avoided asking for accommodation of their needs in the local community which were related to, for instance, their religious beliefs. They did not ask for special arrangements to be made, for example, in restaurants or beauty salons because, as the student cited below explains, they did not want to be perceived to be 'too picky'. Instead the students opted for choices that reduced their levels of anxiety about having to interact in their local communities, but which also meant that they remained 'unnoticed' and their rights and freedoms were even further restricted.

Student: Even when we go to a restaurant we have to ask, is there any animal fat involved in this food. You need to check if it's vegetarian and if it's liquor free, so you feel you're becoming too picky in a way in a restaurant when you ask about the ingredients and everything. And Beauty Salons for example you have to arrange for a place where it's private. If you're doing only your hair, sometimes they don't have private rooms for that, so you have to negotiate. So instead, you go to another beauty salon.

Interviewer: And people may not understand why you have to act like this.

Student: Yes. Yes. (Creative Writing Student, University A)

It was also interesting to note that students accepted discrimination, despite being aware of laws and regulations that could challenge some of the ways in which members of the public 'managed' the presence of international students in local communities. The situation described below refers to renting private accommodation. Despite awareness of their rights to rent, the international student cited below subordinated this right and submitted to the view that him and his family were going to be discriminated because of existing policy rules about renting accommodation to international students. The incident below points to conflicting effects between the stated possibilities and protections international students 'right to rent' may allegedly offer and the student's interpretation of what is *actually* possible. The student's narrative demonstrates their understanding that the 'right to rent' is in fact an abstract right for international students, which never materialises in practice because of the tacit ways this right enables landlords to exercise discrimination. The quote thus evokes interpretations that the ability of an international student to access social benefits is relational and depends, in the first instance, on the official structures that set the conditions for allegedly exercising this ability on equal terms (official 'discursive practice'), but also on tacit discrimination students experience in the everyday, which these structures and policies enable but do not account for (socially manipulated 'discursive practice').

> Student: We couldn't find anything … We went to, we saw the signs [advertising properties to rent], we travelled around and there were like hundreds of signs. We went to these offices [estate agents] and they said, no, we don't have any. But, we told them 'Your …', I mean, there were …
> Interviewer: 'Your sign is just there!'.
> Student: They said 'Oh no, we don't have any …' And somewhere honest with us, they said 'Well, let us be honest with you. Maybe the landlord is not happy to rent the house to an international student'.
> Interviewer: Yes.
> Student: I mean, I could say that … not many were really, they were not interested in like renting their places for students. For, like, a variety of reasons. What were the bad reasons? It could be the nationality.
> Interviewer: But you know that there are laws that give you right to rent?

> Student: Yes, things might be much better in terms of like, legislations, regulations, laws, whatever but, you also deal with the human beings, people do have like, I mean stereotypes. Sometimes misconceptions. (Education Student, University A)

The student explained that it was only in the country of education that they accepted such discrimination, through their own agency that prompted them to subjugate to the penetrating role of regulatory structures and social attitudes, simply because it was just 'easier'. Again, what is evident in the student narrative is that the attitude of 'you also deal with human beings' and making justifications for social stereotyping, whilst offering some sort of comfort to the international student, also makes them more susceptible to the forms of microaggressions they were experiencing, which were legitimised (intentionally or not) by in-country policy agendas related, for instance, to renting accommodation.

Research focusing on international students' experiences from critical race perspectives provides revealing insights into the scope and nature of the type of microaggressions that international students experience, also including those revealed above. It shows that international students encounter 'microinsults', through being subject to a policy environment that conveys insensitivity to their racial and ethnic identity or heritage (e.g. Harper et al. 2016; McGee and Stovall 2015), 'microassaults', which refer to more explicit racial derogation through name calling or overt discriminatory actions (e.g. Brown and Jones 2013) or 'microinvalidations'—that is behaviours that negate and nullify the feelings, knowledge and experiential reality of ethnically diverse persons (e.g. Houshmand et al. 2014; Harwood et al. 2012). 'Microinvalidations' are particularly important for the arguments in this book that are made in Part III, in relation to ways in which the TEF can prevent these microinvalidations through working towards eradicating echoes of coloniality from our teaching practices. But the microaggressions cited above are also highlighted here to once again point out how powerful policies are in determining the reality that may enable these microaggressions to be taking place in the first instance. Microinvalidations, or any type of microaggressions, remind us that even when students attempt to reduce levels of 'suffering' from any type of insults or invalidations, through, for instance, constituting new discursive practices for themselves via subjectivities that emotionally protect them from the effects of discrimination, these discursive practices can never work in their favour because they are constituted in the framework of policies that place social and emotional limitations on international students' lives.

It does not therefore seem that there is any potential for students' subjective interpretations of their reality to supersede the 'actualities' of the reality that are shaped by policies. It seems that it is difficult for 'discursive practices' created by the students, by themselves and for themselves, to have any effects that could produce any complimentary effects or any type of balance that could override the negative effects on international students' lives exerted by official policies. Official rules and regulations always have a bigger bearing. Thus, theorisations which position that there is an equal interplay between formal structures (such as the state, policies, laws, and institutional practices) and self-perceptions of individuals in inscribing power on oneself through emotions (e.g. Ricken 2006), do not seem to adequately capture how little 'wriggle room' international students have, not least as far as their potential to escape the effects of state policies that was revealed above is concerned.

The fact that there is not much international students can do to mitigate the master-processes of 'othering' that are inscribed on them through official policies has not only been established in the UK context, but also internationally. Most international analyses agree that policy regulation is the primary process of control, and anything else, including emotions or even individual efforts or curricular shifts that aim to give international students more equivalence, is limited (e.g. Marginson 2013; McCartney 2016; Matus 2006; França et al. 2018). The emerging role of emotions as a some sort of empowerment, despite sitting comfortably with many poststructuralist perspectives that position individuals as both objects and subjects of experience (e.g. Zembylas 2005; Davids 2014), seems to have little bearing on the negative impacts of policies in the UK and elsewhere (e.g. Lomer 2017; O'Connor 2017). What can, at the very best, be concluded from the review of student emotions presented above is that international students do indeed become engaged with the complex web of power relations, and that, through their emotions, they seek to express themselves against the backdrop of official rules and regulations. Unfortunately, they do not in fact challenge the discriminatory effects of these rules and discourses, because they can't!

Research conducted internationally has shown that international students can't challenge policy hegemony because, through policies, 'governments are assumed to be consistently and intentionally pursuing a positional advantage' (Sá and Sabzalieva 2018, p. 232, also see full article for a review of international students policies from key countries: Australia, Canada, England and the USA). National policies therefore rarely serve the interests of international students and are instead solicited to support national and institutional self-interests. As such, they have the backing from the political power. For instance, differing rules for international students manifested in visa restrictions, additional entry requirements to the country of education or higher fees for the same programmes that home students can access for less money, construct limiting realms of possibilities for international students. These realms stem from the politically motivated priorities, which then create conditions that allow those in authority to explicitly curtail international students' social and personal rights. But in this context, limiting these rights is legitimised by host governments through a rhetoric of protecting public and national interests, which means that actions of governments that may restrict capacities and well-being of international students go unnoticed in the political mainstream or are in fact officially legitimised by the rhetoric of 'doing good' for the country (Hayes 2017). That is why it is extremely difficult for international students to challenge them.

It has long been argued that the degree of limitations policy hegemony can impose on international students depends on individual country differences (Altbach and Knight 2007; Enders 2004; Teichler 2004). This has been argued on the basis that power relations between international students and the state may vary, depending on the characteristics of the socio-political contexts in which these power relations are formed and how, as a result, international students -friendly some countries are. Thus, the socio-political contexts make some countries less disadvantaging for international students than the others (Johnstone and Proctor 2018). But, most analyses also agree that when socio-political contexts and attitudes towards international students change, it is rarely for the benefit of the students, as self-centred priorities of the receiving countries position them mainly as economic objects, vectors of income and sources of institutional prestige (e.g. Paltridge et al. 2014; Schartner and Cho 2017). This positioning does not however mean that international students are suddenly treated better, because they are strategically important for universities. It is in fact the opposite, as policy constructions of them as objects (rather than 'real people') contribute to the absence of any discussions about their human rights. Lack of such discussions and any actions that could guarantee these rights consequently excludes them from equal treatment (e.g. Marginson 2012). In-country priorities therefore make international students 'vulnerable to betrayal in the political games as they become tossed backwards and forwards on the waves of ideological change' (Walker 2014, p. 341).

Graf (2009), for instance, confirms the above observation in his analysis of international students recruitment in the UK and Germany, which is seen by these two countries as the main strategy for internationalisation. Graf (2009) concludes that even those inter-country differences that could afford international students some privileges become blurred in the face of isomorphic pressures of market forces which, if not kept up with, can cause reputational and economic damage to individual countries. These pressures significantly compromise any symbolic in-country differences (and similarities) that could enable epistemic equality for international students. Additionally, as had been argued elsewhere (Hayes 2018), in the context of increasingly marketised attitudes towards internationalisation, gains that come with good 'performance' in the internationalisation category do not require more critical relationships with international students, which could enable their dehumanisation. Thus, political pragmatism underlying internationalisation is unlikely to socialise universities into realising international students as epistemic equals. I have argued elsewhere that even universities with the most conservative cultures and deficit-oriented views on international students, in the climate of current structurally-dominated understandings of internationalisation, can be assessed as 'highly internationalised' (Hayes 2018). Such ratings are possible because high performance in the internationalisation category presently does not require universities to make any changes in how they engage with international students, nor are they required to eradicate pedagogical practices that exclude international students as equals, denying them rights to democratic participation in the classroom.

The recent review of policy and political processes impacting international students in Australia, Canada, the US (also including England) (see Sá and Sabzalieva 2018), or even in Germany, the country known to have the most egalitarian higher education system in the world (Hayes 2019), suggests similar conclusions. Focusing on the question of how public policies in these countries have' dealt with' international students and what factors played a role in establishing certain 'attitudes' towards international students, these reviews generally conclude that internationalisation policies remain highly politicised and give little attention to epistemic democracy for international people. As such, it is not difficult to imagine why democratic realisation of international students plays second fiddle, or in fact has hardly any importance whatsoever. Sá and Sabzalieva (2018), for instance, found that in the US, international student policy has remained closely connected to national security, especially after the 9/11 attack, and to the economic concerns. Such politicisation resulted in most concerns about internationalisation being linked to losing the US's competitive edge (NAFSA Association of International Educators 2007). There is no mention of any attempts to 'better' relationships with international students.

Reviewing the context of Australia, Sá and Sabzalieva (2018) have noted that international students are too mentioned mostly in the context of their benefits to the country's economy, making higher education the country's fourth largest export. Their presence in the Australian context has also been represented elsewhere in rather negative terms, raising questions about the perceived poor learning and language skills and the 'usefulness' of their competencies and qualifications for the Australian labour market (Birrell and Perry 2009). Such highly politicised policy discourses are also said to be linked to the infamous problems of racism, sexual exploitation and crime international students in Australia were experiencing between 2008 and 2009. And it was not until the Chinese and Indian authorities intervened to protect the security of their students, when the Australian government began to talk about international students in terms other than related to the economy (Nyland et al. 2010).

Canada, for instance, while presently perceived to be the most 'international-student friendly' country of education (Bhardwa 2017), has on the other hand been criticised for implementing policies that are 'centred around what makes sense for governments and their bureaucracies', and not being 'centred around international students' (Usher 2016, p. i). Despite immigration policies said to be offering the best 'deal' for international students, in the sense of enabling Express Entry immigration routes (Chiose 2015) and support for permanent residency, the rationales behind these are said to still be highly marketized. It seems that realisation of international students as epistemic equals has not yet found its place in public policies of the country that talks about international students as 'ideal migrants' (Desai-Trilokekar et al. 2016). It might perhaps be because, on the whole, countries around the world are 'embedded in a globally competitive arena for status [which] spurs a conception of internationalisation as instrumental to prestige' (Seeber et al. 2016, p. 698). This book argues that because assessments of this prestige currently do not include any evaluations of *whether* and *how* universities engage with international students in the classroom, commitment to epistemic plurality, in the sense of general agreement that international students' knowledges need to be included as valid and scientific, is not an integral part of university governance and sadly, in many cases, their subordination is still routinely normalised in the everyday.

The subsequent chapters of this book review some research examples which point to tacit ways in which commercialisation of internationalisation contributes to routine normalisation of the processes of subordination international students in UK universities experience. Routine normalisation captures inexplicit power relations that are structured for international students through decision making and strategising that are rationally bounded to internationalisation policies. These policies subsequently dictate what is appropriate and what is presently less important for organisational development (Hayes 2018). As equivalence of international students presently does not bring any 'tangible' institutional benefits, in the same way as increased recruitment of international students or internationally co-authored papers might (as these usually mean higher esteem in national and international rakings), regular and everyday positioning of international students as inferior is therefore unnoticed. International student stories that are revealed later in the book show that their universities do not yet juxtapose their perspectives with those held by home students. To do so, however, would be a primary condition for their inclusion as epistemic equals, predicating an introduction of new pedagogical intentionality that takes account of the relationalities that surround transformation in host communities due to the presence of international students. The philosophical assumptions underlying such pedagogical intentionality are discussed in Chapters 3 and 4. The student narratives cited in the subsequent chapters however show that everything that had happened to students during their time in British classrooms seemed to be unreflectively national in nature and their stories indicate that the students were subject to a nationally normalised education perspective, referred to in this book as 'coloniality'. This seems to suggest that the lack of intentionality to start and maintain equitable and just conditions for inclusion of international students' perspectives is sill characterising higher education teaching, even though universities nowadays are becoming more and more internationalised. This means that international students cannot experience higher education on reciprocal and democratic terms.

Such experiences of higher education will only be possible when they are 'recommended', or even 'mandated' by national policies related to teaching in higher education (I explain the need for 'mandating' this through the TEF in Chapters 3 and 4). As argued above through the review of conceptualisations of 'policy as power', democratisation of university classrooms based on inclusion of international students as equally qualified knowers will only start when it is officially 'measured' in policies. Otherwise, as Chapter 2 reveals in more detail, if policies continue to re-produce constructions of international students based on outdated colonial views, combined with the more recent influence from university rankings, they will simultaneously continue to 'other' them, with some lasting effects. If inclusion of international students as epistemic equals is not part of 'referents' of internationalisation, or 'metrics' that shape understandings of excellence in teaching, then there is no process whereby international students can claim their rights to being treated as 'experts' in the classroom or to re-assert their agency and sense of equality. Such referents therefore are of paramount importance if we want to achieve sector-wide epistemic justice an free from coloniality knowledge production at universities.

Many universities are welcoming and some genuinely engage with cultures and identities of international students. But this is not enough because, at macro-level, through falling in step with policies shaped by commercial rankings and colonial echoes, most see them primarily as economic objects, outsiders, vectors of prestige and beneficiaries of their own prestigious education systems. Naturally, and by extension, they might therefore be reluctant to give international students the same equal status as the home students enjoy. Any attempts towards their more equal inclusion may therefore be limited in the context where nation-state regulations position them as 'other'. Thus, governments who are genuinely committed to ending subordination of international students in the classroom need to correct the divisive boundaries between home and international students through policy objectives that could work towards ending the perpetual superiority of national perspectives in all teaching and learning activities. Policies that include such objectives can lead to significant transformations of intentions.

TEF as a Vehicle for Transformation of Intentions

This book argues that the TEF can be a vehicle through which important transformations in relation to representations of and pedagogical approaches to international students can be effected. The focus on the TEF in the book has been chosen because, as explained through theorisations positioning that policy is power, outlined in the first part of this chapter, a major higher education reform on a national scale such as the TEF can greatly influence ways in which universities work with international students. TEF is also associated with new teaching rankings, which makes the exercise even more powerful. Finally, the TEF is a policy about teaching (at least in principle), which is an area in higher education that has been identified as having the greatest potential to transform the relationships with international students and to ensure their inclusion as equals (e.g. Spiro 2014; Spencer-Oatey and Dauber 2015).

When Crowther and colleagues (2000) discussed the need to consider international students as 'equals' in their seminar work at the European Association for International Education (EAIE) in 2000, they indicated that intercultural practice giving greater equivalence to international students as people in 'their own right' is essential to challenge the systemic marginalisation of this group created by limits of governments' agendas that are driven by self-centered policies and historically-informed attitudes towards foreign people (Crowther et al. 2000). The review of government policies in the UK context, as well as their socio-political undercurrents in Chapter 2, reveals ways in which such marginalisation might be currently occurring in the UK. Chapter 2 also brings to bear ways in which policy representations of international students undermine any reformatory potential of university classrooms. It is argued there, and throughout the book, that the lack of commitment in policies to international people as 'equals' results in universities choosing not to challenge the socio-cultural and educational realities established for them through outdated imperial and colonial views. They don't have to as presently no higher education reform, policy objectives or indeed national or international rankings require them to do so. Instead, the present representations of international students in the TEF as 'deficient' and in need of 'fixing' are rather likely to undermine classroom practice that could lead towards their greater equivalence—the main problem being that such practice does not simply have the 'backing' from the political power.

Despite being British-based, the analysis provided in this book therefore has international implications as it raises important ethical and moral questions about why national evaluations of teaching excellence such as the TEF, and its equivalents around the world (see Chapter 4), do not include any metrics that assess how and whether universities develop critical relationships with international students in the classroom. What is meant by 'critical' is explained in more detail in Chapter 4, but for brevity, it is taken in this book to mean pedagogy that can deliver sustained liberation through the type of classroom activism that liberates the oppressed (international students) and the oppressors (home students) from the damaging effects of coloniality. These effects prevent equivalence of international students' knowledges and limit home students' agency to access the benefits arising from internationalisation. The primary argument in the book therefore is that such metrics should be compulsory, based on the notion that policy can be a means for transformation of intentions (Hall and McGinty 1997). When understood in such terms, policy becomes a conditional matrix consisting of interrelated conditions and their resultant actions and interactions that have specific consequences for the people involved (e.g. Placier et al. 2000). Overall, these conditions produce transformations of intentions because, especially when intended to change something, they contain manifestations of processes that prompt concrete 'human productions in social contexts' (Hall and McGinty 1997, p. 461). These processes are 'entwined not only in issues of content but also in collective perceptions of how to proceed' (ibid., p. 461). Policies therefore transform intentions as they become the field for expressions of new areas for actions, which subsequently foster the contingent and consequential productions that shape progression models and conditions for future activity. Thus, if critical pedagogy with regards to international students is 'made' by the TEF to be a new area for action, it is likely to set conditions for a teaching activity that is geared towards liberation.

The subsequent chapters of the book provide details of this claim and propose a model for a TEF metric that could help to prompt classroom activism that is libertarian in nature. Below, the methodological frame that has shaped the philosophical assumptions underlying the model is outlined first. This methodological frame is based on the previously mentioned approach to discourse and critical policy analysis, the WPR (Bacchi 2009). The approach was suitable to guide the methodology underlying the development of the proposed metric because it is inclusive of notions of power and intentions that are evoked through policies. WPR takes account of these notions through seeking answers to the following analytical questions:

1. What's the problem (here international students and their inclusion) represented to be in a specific policy?
2. What pre-suppositions or assumptions underlie this representation of the 'problem'?
3. How has this representation of the 'problem' come about?

4. What is left unproblematic in this 'problem' representation? Where are the silences? Can the 'problem' be thought about differently?
5. What effects are produced by this representation of the 'problem'?
6. How/where has this representation of the problem been produced, disseminated and defended? How could it be questioned, disrupted and replaced?

The WPR is outlined here, at the start of this book, because it is used in Chapter 2 to interrogate representations of international students that have been lodged within public policies in England. Chapter 2 has been written to provide a clearer understanding of what these policies include with respect to epistemic inclusion of international students and what they leave out. It has also been written to reveal ways in which international students problematisations are central to governing processes at universities. The application of WPR in Chapter 2 also enables an analysis of how what is left unproblematic about international students creates a need for a policy that will encourage their epistemic inclusion. The discussion that is then developed points to ways in which the TEF could prompt new governing processes that could play a role in the process of epistemic inclusion of international students. Based on theorisations about policy as 'discursive practice' developed in this chapter, it is argued that these governing processes will challenge current policy assumptions and pre-suppositions about international students, providing potential for interventions in areas that have so far failed to be problematised.

Applying the WPR makes it possible to see how the model for the new TEF metric proposed in Part III of the book can create representations of international students that are grounded in ideas of epistemic democracy. Firstly, international students will be represented as people in their own right and worthy of equal respect. Secondly, they will be positioned as socially and politically equal experts whose presence can greatly benefit the learning and development of home students. To understand this latter representation, it is important to study Part III of the book which discusses details of the UKES questions that are proposed to be used as the basis for the proposed TEF metric. Based on these questions, and the results presented in Chapter 7, it is argued in this book that the proposed TEF metric can help to free home students from the effects of policy discourses which, through continually questioning the intellectual value of international students, prevent home learners from accessing benefits arising from internationalisation.

Specifically, Chapter 7 reveals that home students presented higher levels of belonging to a classroom community on courses where they were actively encouraged to engage with international students on democratically equal terms. These gains however are not always available to home students as public policies, creating perceptions that international students are inferior, socialise university staff and students into the type of power relations with them that do not challenge traditional social and educational hierarchies (Gorski 2008). Home students therefore, on their own and without the help of their tutors, lack agency to engage with international students on politically and socially equal terms. But it is rarely their fault, as their lack of agency to do so is often restricted by limitations of their own social backgrounds, public discourses about their international colleagues and structural understandings of internationalisation which, shaped by commercial rankings, do not require universities to create conditions for realisation of international students as democratic equals.

But whilst it is obvious that international students' rights to democratic and epistemic inclusion may suffer from such conditions, it is not often considered that home students suffer from such conditions too. But they do, because, as the data modelled in Chapter 7 show, when epistemic inclusion of international students is not practised, benefits of internationalisation are not made available to home students, making their education highly socially unjust. The book therefore argues that there is a need for a TEF metric that will liberate home students from the effects of coloniality—that is, a process which, under the influence of public discourses about international students, has been legitimised to operate based on the logic of cultural, social and political domination over foreign students in an education system (Ghiso and Campano 2013). This process also denies home students access to civic and epistemic development; a situation the proposed metric can change.

As such, the book does not intend to propose metrics that are likely to probe 'pedagogies of reparation'—in the sense that the aim here is not to prompt universities to suddenly start overemphasising identities of international students in the classroom because, they for instance, feel 'guilty' about lack of critical engagement with them or to 'repair' the damage caused by the assumed superiority of home-grown perspectives. When approached from such a perspective, repairing this damage would more likely be related to institutional self-interests, rather than the interests of international students. Rather, the intention of this book is to propose a model for a metric that will prompt genuine commitment to plurality, feeding into the moral and ethical growth of universities that should enter into new social and educational interdependencies with international students. But this requires social and pedagogical changes that accept these students as epistemic equals. Such changes however will only take place if the TEF defends and disseminates them in two ways. One requires inclusion of metrics that can capture the social complexity of intercultural relations in the classroom and *relationality* between these interactions and conditions for inclusion of students as epistemic equals. The second one means a change in the TEF outcomes, from measurements based around benchmarking, which assess outcomes that already exist and are independent of the teaching process, to evaluations that actually focus on fleshing out how much of the outcome of inclusion can be explained by the characteristics of the teaching process. This book is devoted to discussing how such evaluations can be produced, why it is important to produce them and where opportunities for their production lie.

References

Altbach, P. G., & Knight, J. (2007). The internationalization of higher education: Motivations and realities. *Journal of Studies in International Education, 11*(3–4), 290–305.

Bacchi, C. (2009). *Analysing policy: What's the problem represented to be?* Frenchs Forest: Pearson Higher Education.

Bacchi, C., & Bonham, J. (2014). Reclaiming discursive practices as an analytic focus: Political implications. *Foucault Studies, 17,* 179–192.

Ball, S. J. (2012). *Politics and policy making in education: Explorations in sociology*. London. Routledge.

Bhardwa, S. (2017). *Canada is the most popular destination for international students*. Accessed on 4 July 2018. Retrieved from https://www.timeshighereducation.com/student/news/canada-most-popular-destination-international-students.

Birrell, B., & Perry, B. (2009). Immigration policy change and the international student industry. *People and Place, 17*(2), 64–80.

Brown, L., & Jones, I. (2013). Encounters with racism and the international student experience. *Studies in Higher Education, 38*(7), 1004–1019.

Chiose, S. (2015). New immigration rules risk leaving international students behind. *The Globe and Mail*. Retrieved from http://www.theglobeandmail.com/news/national/new-immigration-rules-risk-leavinginternational-students-behind/article22886693.

Crowther, P., Joris, M., Otten, M., Nilsson, B., Teekens, H., & Wächter, B. (2000). *Internationalisation at home: A position paper* (P. Crowther, Ed.). Amsterdam: European Association for International Education.

Davids, M. N. (2014). Using Foucauldian "discursive practices" as conceptual framework for the study of teachers' discourses of HIV and sexuality. *Perspectives in Education, 32*(3), 36–49.

Desai-Trilokekar, R., Thomson, K., & El Masri, A. (2016). *International students as "ideal" immigrants: Ontario employers' perspective*. Accessed on 4 July 2018. Retrieved from https://www.researchgate.net/publication/304039535_International_Students_as_'ideal'_immigrants_Ontario_employers'_perspective.

Enders, J. (2004). Higher education, internationalisation, and the nation-state: Recent developments and challenges to governance theory. *Higher Education, 47*(3), 361–382.

Fischer, F. (2003). *Reframing public policy: Discursive politics and deliberative practices*. Oxford: Oxford University Press.

Foucault, M. (2002). *Archaeology of knowledge*. Abingdon: Routledge.

França, T., Alves, E., & Padilla, B. (2018). Portuguese policies fostering international student mobility: a colonial legacy or a new strategy? *Globalisation, Societies and Education, 16*(3), 325–338.

Ghiso, M. P., & Campano, G. (2013). Coloniality and education: Negotiating discourses of immigration in schools and communities through border thinking. *Equity & Excellence in Education, 46*(2), 252–269.

Gorski, P. C. (2008). Good intentions are not enough: A decolonizing intercultural education. *Intercultural education, 19*(6), 515–525.

Graf, L. (2009). Applying the varieties of capitalism approach to higher education: Comparing the internationalisation of German and British universities. *European Journal of Education, 44*(4), 569–585.

Hall, P. M., & McGinty, P. J. (1997). Policy as the transformation of intentions: Producing program from statute. *Sociological Quarterly, 38*(3), 439–467.

Harper, S. R., Davis, C. F., & Smith, E. J. (2016). A critical race case analysis of black undergraduate student success at an urban university. *Urban Education, 53*(1), 3–25.

Harwood, S. A., Huntt, M. B., Mendenhall, R., & Lewis, J. A. (2012). Racial microaggressions in the residence halls: Experiences of students of color at a predominantly White university. *Journal of Diversity in Higher Education, 5*(3), 159–173.

Hayes, A. (2017). Why international students have been "TEF-ed out"? *Educational Review, 69*(2), 218–231.

Hayes, A. (2018). Nation boundedness and international students' marginalisation: What's emotion got to do with it? *International Studies in Sociology of Education*. http://dx.doi.org/10.1080/09620214.2018.1453305.

Hayes, A. (2019). 'We loved it because we felt that we existed there in the classroom!': International students as epistemic equals versus double-country oppression. *Journal of Studies in International Education*. https://doi.org/10.1177/1028315319826304.

Houshmand, S., Spanierman, L. B., & Tafarodi, R. W. (2014). Excluded and avoided: Racial microaggressions targeting Asian international students in Canada. *Cultural Diversity and Ethnic Minority Psychology, 20*(3), 377–388.

Johnstone, C., & Proctor, D. (2018). Aligning institutional and national contexts with internationalization efforts. *Innovative Higher Education, 43*(1), 5–16.

Lomer, S. (2017). Soft power as a policy rationale for international education in the UK: A critical analysis. *Higher Education, 74*(4), 581–598.

Marginson, S. (2012). Including the other: Regulation of the human rights of mobile students in a nation-bound world. *Higher Education, 63*(4), 497–512.

Marginson, S. (2013). Equals or others? Mobile students in a nationally bordered world. In S. Sovic & M. Blythman (Eds.), *International students negotiating higher education* (pp. 9–27). London: Routledge.

Matus, C. (2006). Interrupting narratives of displacement: International students in the United States. *Perspectives in Education, 24*(4), 81–92.

McCartney, D. M. (2016). Inventing international students: Exploring discourses in international student policy talk, 1945–75. *Historical Studies in Education/Revue d'histoire de l'éducation, 28*(2), 1–27.

McGee, E. O., & Stovall, D. (2015). Reimagining critical race theory in education: Mental health, healing, and the pathway to liberatory praxis. *Educational Theory, 65*(5), 491–511.

NAFSA Association of International Educators. (2007). *Why America needs an international education policy*. Washington, DC: NAFSA Association of International Educators.

Nyland, C., Forbes-Mewett, H., & Marginson, S. (2010). The international student safety debate: Moving beyond denial. *Higher Education Research & Development, 29*(1), 89–101.

O'Connor, S. (2017). Problematising strategic internationalisation: Tensions and conflicts between international student recruitment and integration policy in Ireland. *Globalisation, Societies and Education, 16,* 1–14.

Paltridge, T., Mayson, S., & Schapper, J. (2014). Welcome and exclusion: An analysis of The Australian newspaper's coverage of international students. *Higher Education, 68*(1), 103–116.

Placier, M., Hall, P. M., McKendall, S. B., & Cockrell, K. S. (2000). Policy as the transformation of intentions: Making multicultural education policy. *Educational Policy, 14*(2), 259–289.

Ricken, N. (2006). The power of power—Questions to Michel Foucault. *Educational Philosophy and Theory, 38*(4), 541–560.

Sá, C. M., & Sabzalieva, E. (2018). The politics of the great brain race: Public policy and international student recruitment in Australia, Canada, England and the USA. *Higher Education, 75*(2), 231–253.

Schartner, A., & Cho, Y. (2017). 'Empty signifiers' and 'dreamy ideals': Perceptions of the 'international university' among higher education students and staff at a British university. *Higher Education, 74*(3), 455–472.

Seeber, M., Cattaneo, M., Huisman, J., & Paleari, S. (2016). Why do higher education institutions internationalize? An investigation of the multilevel determinants of internationalization rationales. *Higher Education, 72*(5), 685–702.

Spencer-Oatey, H., & Dauber, D. (2015). *How internationalised is your university?* UKCISA Occasional Paper. Accessed on 26 June 2016. Retrieved from http://institutions.ukcisa.org.uk/Info-for-universities-colleges–schools/Publications–research/resources/84/How-internationalised-is-your-university.

Spiro, J. (2014). Learning interconnectedness: Internationalisation through engagement with one another. *Higher Education Quarterly, 68*(1), 65–84.

Taylor, S. (2004). Researching educational policy and change in 'new times': Using critical discourse analysis. *Journal of Education Policy, 19*(4), 433–451.

Teichler, U. (2004). The changing debate on internationalisation of higher education. *Higher Education, 48*(1), 5–26.

Thomson, P., Hall, C., & Jones, K. (2013). Towards educational change leadership as a discursive practice—Or should all school leaders read Foucault? *International Journal of Leadership in Education, 16*(2), 155–172.

Usher, A. (2016). *A new logo for Canadian higher education.* Accessed on 4 July 2018. Retrieved from http://higheredstrategy.com/a-newlogo-for-canadian-higher-education/.

Walker, P. (2014). International student policies in UK higher education from colonialism to the coalition: Developments and consequences. *Journal of Studies in International Education, 18*(4), 325–344.

Young, R. (Ed.). (1987). *Untying the text: A post-structuralist reader.* Boston: Routledge & Kegan Paul.

Zembylas, M. (2005). Discursive practices, genealogies, and emotional rules: A poststructuralist view on emotion and identity in teaching. *Teaching & Teacher Education: An International Journal of Research and Studies, 21*(8), 935–948.

2

Policy Representations of International Students in the UK

This chapter reviews policy representations of international students in the UK, evoking imperial echoes, which in later years translated into constructions of international students as people who are educationally and culturally inferior. Two key arguments are made in relation to the role of the TEF in changing these constructions. The first one posits that if the TEF does not include a new metric assessing the type of teaching that will 'obligate' universities to realise international students as epistemic 'equals', their status quo as 'inferiors' will be maintained. The second argument asserts that through this new metric, the TEF could create opportunities for assessments of internationalisation that are distanced from historical and socio-political influences that have produced uneven lines of global connection at universities which are revealed in the extracts from the interviews with the students cited towards the end of the chapter.

International students recruitment to the UK is not a new phenomenon. It started during the British colonial period and had a mainly 'developmental' character, as it was seen by the British to be a way of gaining control of trade, through fashioning what and how colonial students studied (Pietsch 2012). Macaulay (1835, p. i), for instance,

© The Author(s) 2019
A. Hayes, *Inclusion, Epistemic Democracy and International Students,*
https://doi.org/10.1007/978-3-030-11401-5_2

29

noted that through mandating British education in Indian colonies, the British aimed to establish their dominion through education, by creating "a class of persons, Indian in blood and colour, but English in taste, in opinions, in morals, and in intellect". Pietsch (2012) has subsequently argued that such colonial history manifests itself in attitudes towards and pitfalls of internationalisation today.

One of these pitfalls seems to be the perceived superiority of the British education over those acquired in other nations. By mandating British education in former colonies, colonial governments institutionalised this superiority, rationalising the expansion of the British system abroad as a necessary process of 'enlightenment' to international people (Walker 2014). By extension, students began to receive British education in the former colonies, through the University of London's external examination system which enabled colonial students to gain a degree by taking London examinations locally (Clover 2012). The system was however quickly discovered not to be cost effective—which resulted in relocation of colonial students to England—a strategy that was disadvantaging for colonial students as they had increasingly been faced with racism and abuse on arrival in England (e.g. Williams 1990). Colonial echoes are also said to be disadvantaging international students nowadays, as they have contributed to shaping current perceptions of international students as 'immigrants' and 'supplicants' (e.g. Madge et al. 2009).

Holding fully established beliefs that British education was superior, however, many colonial students were keen to re-locate to England. The prestige attached to English degrees and the obligation to have them for certain civil service positions, as well as emerging views that degrees gained in students' own countries, despite being awarded by British universities, did not have equal value to those awarded in London, prompted increased numbers of international students to go to England (Walker 2014). A number of these students were supported by scholarships from colonial governments, but these were limited, pushing those students who received them to live in poverty and those who didn't to rely on the welfare system of the host country. The additional cost for the British state connected with supporting newly arriving students, the shortage of housing that was linked to their increased numbers, reductions to some community services, as well as the 'alien'

2 Policy Representations of International Students in the UK 31

skin colour of foreign students had led to public hostility towards them (Walker 2014).

Despite such accounts, and influenced by the imperial echoes that continue to emphasise the prestige of the British education system (HM Government 2013), many international students continue to arrive in Britain, with fully established intentions to use English degrees as a vehicle for status sorting at home (e.g. Gu and Schweisfurth 2015). Recent research also suggests that, to an extent, they are even prepared to accept discrimination, as they understand it as 'part and parcel' of being an outsider and because they see their presence in the country of education as transitional (Hayes 2018). It has been pointed out that 'ways in which international students understand themselves in relation to the country of education and how their subjective interpretations of "self" as temporary outsiders, fed by complementary long-term imaginaries of their futures beyond the present context of education, make a difference to the ways they deal with discrimination' (Hayes 2018, p. 300). This, however, does not change the fact that they continue to be discriminated through the impact of imperial echoes, which have prompted British governments over the years to create differing rules for their participation in the British education system. These rules exclude them from accessing the same benefits as home students for the same moral and monetary price and create barriers between 'us' and 'them', with ethical consequences preventing realisation of international students as epistemic 'equals' in the classroom.

The case of differing fees is probably one of the most illustrative examples of the ways in which the questions of ethics are not addressed when it comes to 'managing' the flows of international students. The lack of attention to these questions limits opportunities for their democratic participation in the classroom. When growing international students numbers studying for free, especially after World War 2, began to be seen as causing strains on the higher education system, which was no longer able to subsidise their living and studying costs, in 1967 Britain moved from a system of funding overseas students based on public subsidies to a strategy based on higher fees for international students (Bolsmann and Miller 2008). It has been argued that through this move, the nation created a form of dualism in higher education that separated home and international students into 'us' and 'them' (Silver and Silver 1997). Additionally, more international student limits were introduced in 1977 to further reduce the amount of subsidy for international students, whereby quota limits were introduced as a way of reducing international enrolments (Williams 1984). The biggest change, however, came in 1980 when Britain introduced a full-cost policy for overseas students, meaning that full fees had to be paid by international students and all grant support from British institutions was removed (Williams 1984). These changes have subsequently 'sent shock waves through a number of Britain's international relationships' and 'severely affected the flow of students… and promoted re-evaluation of policy towards overseas students' (Overseas Students Trust 1987, cited in Bolsmann and Miller 2008, p. 4). They have also neglected to address ethical questions of how these changes were going to problematise the presence of international students in Britain. We know today that they have contributed to their constructions as 'economic objects' (Lomer 2014), silencing any discussions about them as people worthy of equal respect.

Representations of international students as economic objects and the absence of any discussions regarding the ethical implications of such representations have been sustained in government policies in later years as well. Tony Blair, as leader of the Labour party that succeeded the Conservative government responsible for the full cost international students policy, was particularly focused on more 'energetic' recruitment of international students as a means to economic growth. In this regard, Blair introduced policies known as the Prime Minister's Initiatives (PMI), under which entry procedures for international students and work rules were streamlined to enable the benefits international students could offer for British commercial interests (Blair's speech 1999). It should also, however, be noted that under Tony Blair, discourses about fostering intercultural connection with international students were more prominent than under any other government and Blair actually commissioned a number of projects looking into improving international students experience in Britain (Li-Hua et al. 2011).

The Coalition government that succeeded Labour in 2010 officially ended PMI and instead published the International Education Strategy (IES) in 2013 which focused primarily on income from education

2 Policy Representations of International Students in the UK 33

exports and soft power opportunities abroad available through international students. The strategy highlighted UK's history and brand, as well as the country's leading position in international education as assets benefiting international students and countries abroad (HM Government 2013). The Coalition also toughened up immigration rules streamlined by Labour, re-introducing, for instance, border interviews and ending the right to work for international students post study. International students thus continued to be represented as economic objects whose value to the UK lied mainly in monetary terms. Additionally, growing discourses of English education as an 'asset' contributed to their representations as 'inferiors', as political rhetoric of helping those less fortunate through expansion of British education featured strongly in the IES strategy. Under Coalition, university ministers also wanted more scrutiny over the 'value' of international students to the UK, with Damian Green, then the immigration minister, suggesting that 'expanding the number of international students in the UK is not necessarily a good thing' (Grove 2012, p. i).

The context of wider discussions about the threats of immigration contributed to public representations of international students as 'abusers' of the British education and immigration system, which resulted in 'a drive to stop bogus colleges and bogus students' from coming to the UK and to ensure that 'only high-quality genuine students can come to the UK to study with legitimate education providers' (Damian Green, cited in Grove 2012, p. i). This drive was influenced by advice from the Migration Advisory Committee (MAC) who suggested that 'there is scope for further examination of whether and to what extent foreign student tuition fees boost the UK economy and, crucially, how UK residents ultimately benefit from that' (Grove 2012, p. i). Such government rhetoric implying that international students may be negatively affecting the wellbeing of UK residents was hardly going to prompt public intentions to treat them as epistemic equals.

The Conservative government that succeeded the Coalition in 2015 further restricted international students visa licences to only 'high quality' universities. These restrictions were said to be a 'cover for wanting to stop anyone else from coming [to the UK]' (Hillman 2016, p. 26). They were also said to reflect a step back from an international to increasingly national system of HE, 'to help British people succeed in life' (ibid., p. 26). Representations of international students affecting life opportunities of the nationals, as well as the quality of higher education, were carried through in the next manifesto issued by the party in 2017, which pledged to 'toughen the visa requirements for students, to make sure that we maintain high standards' (The Conservative Manifesto 2017, p. 54). This pledge was also included under the section on immigration, representing international students as those 'unruly' migrants that come to the UK to abuse the system. That is why the party pledged that 'we will expect students to leave the country at the end of their course, unless they meet new, higher requirements that allow them to work in Britain after their studies have concluded' (The Conservative Manifesto 2017, p. 54). The manifesto continued that 'overseas students will remain in the immigration statistics – in line with international definitions – and within scope of the government's policy to reduce annual net migration' (ibid., pp. 54–55). Despite numerous warnings that keeping international students in immigration quotas could have negative effects on their representations and perceptions that they are not welcome in Britain (e.g. Lord Bilimoria's speech 2016), which were even issued by the Prime Minister's own home secretary, Amber Rudd (Parker and Warrell 2017), the Conservatives decided to continue to keep international students in the migration figures.

The most recent Higher Education Bill, and especially the TEF (which the Bill introduces) can also be seen to be shaping representations of international students that are likely to limit their equal and epistemic rights. There is an overwhelming absence of any plans to include international students in the TEF, in the sense of people whose realisation in the classroom as epistemic equals could be seen as a unique teaching skills (Hayes 2017). Instead, where they are mentioned, the exercise constructs them as commercial objects, consumers and people in education deficit (more details are provided in Chapter 5). This denies them equal rights as 'objects', that have no soul, as the logic would suggest, do not tend to need them. But this book argues that the TEF can transform representations of international students, but, as will be explained in subsequent chapters, it first needs to include metrics that will set conditions for their representations as people

2 Policy Representations of International Students in the UK 35

worthy of equal respect. Through such metrics, the TEF will then be able to 'cushion', and hopefully with time eradicate, the negative effects of policy representations discussed in this chapter so far. As alluded to in Chapter 1, the book focuses on the TEF that can effect such a change because (a) in principle, the TEF is meant to evaluate teaching, and teaching has been identified as an area that has the potential to transform relationships with international students and (b) because national policies on the scale of the TEF (functioning as a 'discursive practice') can prompt more inclusive attitudes towards international students at universities, especially if commitment to plurality becomes one of the key determinants that is measured by national rankings.

Yet international students are not represented in the TEF as worthy of equal respect. Instead, their positioning in any TEF consultations extends from the old imperial influences and depends on selective attention to celebrating only certain types of diversity—that is, those that are politically important and ones that can help fulfil politicised objectives created under the 'common good' agendas (understood as contributing to people's agency via supporting their civic development and social welfare—e.g. Leal 2017). The types of diversity that are currently highlighted in the TEF are mostly related to working class students and other widening participation groups (e.g. students with disabilities, mature students or Black and Minority Ethnic groups). This book does not dispute the importance of inclusion of these diverse groups, but it additionally asks why inclusion of international students is not represented as contributing to common good as well? Part III of the book will show ways in which inclusion of international students as epistemic equals can also contribute to civic development and wellbeing of home students. In this sense, this development could also be understood as 'common good' as it can help home students unlock the benefits of internationalisation. It is thus urged here that the TEF should be committed to evaluating teaching activism which creates situations in which international and home students can be reciprocally positioned as 'equals'. When inclusion of international students operates on such terms, universities can then learn how, through complimentary effects of such positioning, they can fulfil their social responsibilities, not only towards international students but also towards the home ones.

36   A. Hayes

For the time being, however, universities are still found to be creating conditions that exclude rather than include international students. In most cases, if not all, this is probably not intentional but is rather an unintended consequence of policies that socialise universities into particular ways of thinking about the presence of border-crossing people in higher education. One of these consequences is the idea that international students' learning cultures need to be 'corrected', in order for them to succeed in the British system (e.g. Lillyman and Bennett 2014; Mwale et al. 2018). Such problematisations give rise to previously mentioned coloniality of knowledge, which essentially means the hegemony and prevalence of Western knowledge as normative and incorporation of all other forms of knowledge into this single norm (e.g. Baker 2012). Coloniality therefore prevents critical engagement with international students because it is based on the presumption of a 'single path of human progress and of the universal value of Western knowledge' (Stein et al. 2016, p. 4). Consequently, alternative perspectives of knowledge and modes of learning are viewed as 'inferior' and behind the Anglophone countries in time. This creates a prescription in education discourses that international students must be continually 'upskilled' (Da Silva 2015). This prescription is then justified based on notions of 'conditional equality'—that is, others can also be equal as long as their deficits are fixed (ibid.). Marginson (2013) refers to this prescription as cultural domination, arguing that:

> It is assumed that the host country culture normalised by this prescription remains unchanged. The international student 'adjusts' to the host nation but not vice versa. Adjustment is 'successful' to the extent students discard their beliefs and adopt values and behaviours of host-country norms. The idea of one way adjustment implies the host culture is superior, fitting popular prejudices. (Marginson 2013, p. 12)

Popular prejudices therefore reinforce representations of the countries of education as superior and international students as lacking moral and intellectual capacity. Such views also set in motion specific ways of working with international students that are based mainly around remedial support and premised on the colonial tenets of 'civilising' and

2 Policy Representations of International Students in the UK   37

helping those less able (Kapoor 2014). These, in turn, affect the manner in which international students in host countries are approached and internalised into classroom communities. The excerpts cited below, from interviews with international students that were conducted as part of the broader research underling this book, provide some relevant insights.

For example, the interview with the student cited below reveals ways in which monocultural diet of curricula at British universities imposed conditions of (de-) participation on that student in the classroom. This monocultural teaching limited that student's capacity and opportunities to contribute to discussions. It is revealed below that the limitations imposed on the student through an explicitly British content of the material in the student's classes excluded any possibility of them being perceived as 'equals' and 'experts'. Instead, the focus of the materials created feelings of alienation and perception of that student that they could never fully be part of conventional learning in their classes. The teacher behaviour captured in the student's narrative also demonstrates that the knowledge that the student had contributed did not seem to equally intersect with the knowledge that was collectively produced by the British students. This encouraged the home students to assume an elitist position over the student in question. ('S' refers to the student, 'I' to the interviewer).

S: Sometimes, I feel like I want to say something but then I don't really have the chance to speak in the…like … seminars and …
I: Why did you feel you didn't have a chance?
S: I don't know. I think people are just, like, talking like they were… And then, I felt like I have opinion about it as well. But then maybe sometimes, I don't have the chance to say it (…) Because I feel like people who are brilliant in Politics talk so much. And then, we [international students] stay quiet, and then we just…We, like, nodding and …
I: So…And you stayed quiet because you are an international student? Is it what you are saying?
S: Yes, kind of.
I: Yes, okay. And that was because you didn't have the answer or there are other reasons for it?
S: Sometimes, because I didn't really know the answer. And then, I just felt like, maybe others, they all know about it and I don't really know about it. And then, the teacher have to pick me about the question (…)

38   A. Hayes

Because most of the curriculums and policies we learn about is more UK-based. And then, I don't really know about the, like... For example, one incident happened and then this policy came up. And then, how the whole system works and...Yes.

I: When you recall that situation when the teacher called your name because they wanted you to answer, what did you do then?

S: I just smiled. I think that's what most international students do. It was... Yes.

I: And what did the teacher do?

S: The teacher would be, like, 'Oh just say your opinion and it's fine' [mimicking teacher's dismissive attitude]. And then I was, like, 'Oh I don't really know what to say' but then I would just say something and then the teacher would go on to the next [student]. (…) I felt, like, they [home students] engaged more with the teacher. Like, the teacher will be more...Like, when the teacher asked me questions, I felt like my answers are not really valuable … Yes, as much as …

I: As the others.

S: Yes.

The interview extract that is cited next also suggests ways in which coloniality can additionally be manifested in broader approaches to teaching and learning. The logic of educational domination of the 'British' ways of learning leads to setting these ways as normative and as the only viable pathway to educational success. This positioning also has an effect on the students, who consequently marginalise the status of the ways of learning developed in their home countries and think of these ways as 'inferior'. Such thinking instils a sense of 'responsibilisation' in the students, who make themselves responsible for discarding home country ways of learning.

S: My first lecturer, he didn't teach, in my opinion, he didn't teach, he asked questions, again and again, and I said, and I thought that he didn't teach because in my country the teacher explained. Like a very long explanation.

I: What were you feeling? Do you remember?

S: At that time I felt that I was afraid. I started to feel afraid. Of being not able to, like keep up with the lectures and also I am, I was so afraid

2 Policy Representations of International Students in the UK   39

that I cannot catch up with my peers (…) But this is my own problem. So, it's only my problem I think. Because it is a different academic background, culture and so it is me the one who has to adjust with the culture here. So I think the way you study here, those are things that I have to follow.

The final quote below reflects the colonial prescription that legitimises approaches to domination of international students, through a rhetoric of conditional equality. The student quoted below recalled that their university would not even accept the fact that their English language ability was not a problem and that they might have already been introduced to some of the education standards of writing essays that are required at English universities. Assumptions that they were deficient resulted in multiple referrals of that student to remedial classes, which became part of the everyday actions that underlined the interactions with this student at their university. These referrals were derogatory for the student in both, academic and moral terms.

> *S*: [in the remedial workshop] they told me something I already knew, like, you need to have introduction. And you need to have a main body. And you need to have a conclusion. That is something everybody kind of knows, before coming to Uni, already. (…) What they offered wasn't really helpful. Because I took one in my first year, and I took another one in my second year. I actually expected I could gain a little bit of help from there. But then, the module context was completely the same from first year to second year. It was just paraphrasing, like, it was just…I remember, like, for both years, what we learned, like, in the first lecture was the same thing and it was the same Power Point. I didn't learn … at the beginning, I felt like maybe language is really the barrier. And then, I felt like it's not … And then, I just felt, like, what's the point of taking it?

It has already been observed elsewhere that remedial classes, although well-meaning, often marginalise the position of international students as 'equals' because attending them is automatically associated with being 'deficient' (e.g. Sutherland et al. 2015). And those who are 'deficient' cannot possibly be 'experts'. It has also been observed that these classes seek to turn international students into learners who can eventually display the same characteristics as the students in the country of education (e.g. Marginson 2013). However, the quotes from the students in German universities that are cited below also reveal that coloniality, whether manifested through 'reparation of' or 'domination over' international students' national and educational characteristics, extends beyond views and skills shaped nationally in countries of education. The quotes below show that students are expected not only to display the characteristics of the countries of education but also (and perhaps predominantly so) to display characteristics of Anglophone learners, *despite* studying in a non-Anglophone country. This seems to suggest that coloniality is a cross-border hegemony, which evolves under conditions that reflect some sort of 'double-country oppression' (Hayes 2019). 'Double-country oppression' excludes international students through actions that do not necessarily aim to strengthen the position of the German view on education but rather reinforce (most likely unintentionally) the dominant position of the Anglophone view. The evidence given by the students thus implies that 'coloniality' is less of an issue of geopolitics and more of an issue of global university competition that evolves under Anglophone perspectives and that is planetary in scale. This evidence supports Mignolo (2003) who notes that local perspectives are everywhere but that only *some* local perspectives are in a position of imagining and shaping global views on what 'counts', for example, in education. This threatens possibilities for more epistemic inclusion of international students that could be offered by inter-country differences and how these differences influence their representations. The quotes below reflect this threat, showing ways in which, despite Germany's more inclusive policy discourses surrounding the presence of international students than in England (Hillman 2015), national universities follow global actors who already hold privileging positions.

> *S*: The Germans want to know more about students who are English, or I don't know, Canadian, but for the Italians, they are just an international student; not only the Italians but also South Korean, Chinese, all the others.
> *S*: During the course, I had a really bad situation with the teacher, she was giving attention only to American and Canadian students, without

2 Policy Representations of International Students in the UK 41

considering the others. During the course, the American and Canadian students did not say anything to other international students and the teacher said 'Oh maybe because you don't understand anything, so maybe this course is not for you'. So she made me feel like I was not at the level of the course. I felt excluded of course, because I never thought I was not at the level of the others! This teacher, throughout this course, always continued to have the same attitude, she always asked the American girl, the Canadian girl, let's say, English speakers but the others, she didn't really care. I was shocked because hm … it was the course for people who speak other languages, so I thought that was the course that didn't have to deal with those kind of issues.

In summary, two broad understandings of the ways in which realisation of international students as epistemic equals is affected in countries of education emerge in this chapter. The first one seems to be focused on national policy effects, and provides support for Williams's (1984) arguments that once policies establish the status quo of international students, it is difficult to change. The second one draws attention to the global influence of the Anglophone position. The whole purpose of this book is to however show that realisation of international students as equals does not have to rest on either the historical and socio-political influences of countries of education, or does it have to have anything to do with the dominant position of some countries that produce uneven lines of global connection at universities. The subsequent chapters present ways in which both of these 'types' of influences can be reduced through adequate changes to teaching assessments such as the TEF. These changes are likely to prompt ways that will enable universities to distance themselves from the damaging effects of the outdated political views on attitudes towards international students and from the dominance of the Anglophone actors. The book proposes changes in the TEF outcomes that are less likely to be politicised, as they will focus purely on the interdependence between inclusion of international students and the characteristics of pedagogy. It is true that pedagogy can also be politicised, of course, especially when it comes to multiculturalism and inclusion (e.g. Giroux 2000), but if the *relationality* between inclusion and the teaching process is set to be the main outcome that is 'measured', without any set standards or cut off points indicating of what this outcome should be, and adjusting for any contextual factors that could affect said relationality, then the political influence is reduced as all assessments are based purely on performance according to each classroom's specifications (details of this claim are provided in Parts II and III of this book). Measuring performance according to own specifications can be rather *apolitical*.

By extension, the proposed changes to the TEF should therefore prompt pedagogies that are less likely to be influenced by the pursuit of the Anglophone knowledge, as they will create assessment criteria requiring universities to demonstrate non-hierarchical commitment to *all* students. Such criteria will no longer allow for discrimination of certain groups and favouring of others to go unnoticed in the political spectrum, as universities will be assessed on how teaching creates situations in which Anglophone (be it home or international learners) and non-Anglophone students are interchangeably positioned as either 'experts' or 'others'. These new criteria will above all assess how complimentary effects of such positioning can lead to democratic life of students and pedagogical intentionality that supports this life. Yet, such criteria are not considered in any international proposals for assessments of teaching at universities. The second part of the book provides more details of the ways they have been left out in major teaching excellence projects around the world. Part II also deconstructs how this may be seen to be linked to the conditionality that characterises relationships with international students in higher education, which is subsequently deconstructed as a veiled continuation of coloniality.

References

Baker, M. (2012). Modernity/coloniality and Eurocentric education: Towards a post-occidental self-understanding of the present. *Policy Futures in Education, 10*(1), 4–22.

Blair, T. (1999, June 18). *Attracting more international students* [Speech to London School of Economics launching Prime Minister's Initiative].

Accessed on 5 July 2018. Retrieved from http://webarchive.nationalarchives. gov.uk/20070701135817/http://www.pm.gov.uk/output/Page3369.asp.

Bolsmann, C., & Miller, D. R. (2008). International student recruitment to universities in England: Discourse, rationales and globalisation. *Globalisation, Societies & Education, 6*(1), 75–88.

Clover, D. (2012, July 4–6). *Special relations: The University of London and the University College of the West Indies.* Paper delivered at the 36th Annual Conference of the Society for Caribbean Studies, Rewley House and Kellogg College, University of Oxford.

Da Silva, D. F. (2015). Globality. *Critical Ethnic Studies, 1*(1), 33–38.

Giroux, H. A. (2000). Racial politics, pedagogy, and the crisis of representation in academic multiculturalism. *Social Identities, 6*(4), 493–510.

Grove, J. (2012). Immigration minister wants more scrutiny of 'value' of foreign students. *Times Higher Education.* Accessed on 5 July 2018. Retrieved from https://www.timeshighereducation.com/news/immigration-minister-wants-more-scrutiny-of-value-of-foreign-students/418924.article.

Gu, Q., & Schweisfurth, M. (2015). Transnational connections, competences and identities: Experiences of Chinese international students after their return 'home'. *British Educational Research Journal, 41*(6), 947–970.

Hayes, A. (2017). The teaching excellence framework in the United Kingdom: An opportunity to include international students as "equals"? *Journal of Studies in International Education, 21*(5), 483–497.

Hayes, A. (2018). Nation boundedness and international students' marginalisation: What's emotion got to do with it? *International Studies in Sociology of Education, 27*(2–3), 288–306.

Hayes, A. (2019). 'We loved it because we felt that we existed there in the classroom!': International students as epistemic equals versus double-country oppression. *Journal of Studies in International Education.* https://doi. org/10.1177/1028315319826304.

Hillman, N. (2015). *Keeping up with the Germans? A comparison of student funding, internationalisation and research in UK and German universities.* Oxford, England: Higher Education Policy Institute.

Hillman, N. (2016, October 13). The UK government's latest baad idea: Sorting sheep from goats. *Times Higher Education,* no. 2, 276.

HM Government. (2013). *International education: Global growth and prosperity.* Accesses on 5 July 2018. Retrieved from https://assets.publishing. service.gov.uk/government/uploads/system/uploads/attachment_data/ file/340600/bis-13-1081-international-education-global-growth-and-prosperity-revised.pdf.

Kapoor, I. (2014). Psychoanalysis and development: Contributions, examples, limits. *Third World Quarterly, 35,* 1120–1143.

Leal, M. N. (2017). Commodity versus common good: Internationalization in Latin-American higher education. In *BCES Conference Books* (Vol. 15). Sofia: Bulgarian Comparative Education Society.

Li-Hua, R., Wilson, J., Aouad, G., & Li, X. (2011). Strategic aspects of innovation and internationalization in higher education: The Salford PMI2 experience. *Journal of Chinese Entrepreneurship, 3*(1), 8–23.

Lillyman, S., & Bennett, C. (2014). Providing a positive learning experience for international students studying at UK universities: A literature review. *Journal of Research in International Education, 13*(1), 63–75.

Lomer, S. (2014). Economic objects: How policy discourse in the United Kingdom represents international students. *Policy Futures in Education, 12*(2), 273–285.

Lord Bilimoria of Chelsea. (2016, November 17). *Speech—Immigration: Overseas students.* Accessed on 5 July 2018. Retrieved from http://www.lord-bilimoria.co.uk/speech-immigration-overseas-students/.

Macaulay, T. B. (1835). Minute by the Hon'ble. In H. Sharp (Ed.), *Bureau of education: Selections from educational records, Part I (1781–1839)* (pp. 107–117). Calcutta: Superintendent, Government Printing, 1920. Reprint. Delhi: National Archives of India, 1965.

Madge, C., Raghuram, P., & Noxolo, P. (2009). Engaged pedagogy and responsibility: A postcolonial analysis of international students. *Geoforum, 40*(1), 34–45.

Marginson, S. (2013). Equals or others? Mobile students in a nationally bordered world. In S. Sovic & M. Blythman (Eds.), *International students negotiating higher education* (pp. 9–27). London: Routledge.

Mignolo, W. (2003). Globalization and the geopolitics of knowledge: The role of the humanities in the corporate university. *Nepantla: Views from South 4*(1), 97–119.

Mwale, S., Alhawsawi, S., Sayed, Y., & Rind, I. A. (2018). Being a mobile international postgraduate research student with family in the United Kingdom: Conflict, contestation and contradictions. *Journal of Further & Higher Education, 42*(3), 301–312.

Parker, G. & Warrell. H. (2017). Amber Rudd urges removal of students from net migration data. *The Financial Times* [online]. Accessed 5 July 2018. Retrieved from https://www.ft.com/content/1c51a9dc-c3c3-11e7-a1d2-6786f39ef675.

Pietsch, T. (2012). Imperial echoes. *Times Higher Education*, no. 2040, 41–45. Education Abstracts.

Silver, H., & Silver, P. (1997). *Students: Changing roles, changing lives*. Buckingham: Open University Press.

Stein, S., Andreotti, V. D. O., & Suša, R. (2016). 'Beyond 2015', within the modern/colonial global imaginary? Global development and higher education. *Critical Studies in Education*, 1–21. https://doi.org/10.1080/1750848 7.2016.1247737.

Sutherland, A., Edgar, D., & Duncan, P. (2015). International infusion in practice—From cultural awareness to cultural intelligence. *Journal of Perspectives in Applied Academic Practice, 3*(3), 32–40.

The Conservative Manifesto. (2017). *Forward together: Our plan for a stronger Britain and a prosperous future*. Accessed on 11 July 2018. Retrieved from https://www.conservatives.com/manifesto.

Walker, P. (2014). International student policies in UK higher education from colonialism to the coalition: Developments and consequences. *Journal of Studies in International Education, 18*(4), 325–344.

Williams, P. (1984). Britain's full-cost policy for overseas students. *Comparative Education Review, 28*(2), 258–278.

Williams, L. (1990). *Country studies on student mobility*. London, UK: Overseas Students Trust.

Part II

Teaching Excellence in Higher Education and Internationalisation

3

Conditionality as a Veiled Continuation of Coloniality vs. Epistemic Democracy

This chapter brings together key theorisations about coloniality in higher education. It draws on the notion of inclusion of international students in the host country education system as being based on conditional equality (i.e. others can also be equal as long as they discard their own ways of knowing) to point out ways in which this type of conditionality reflects a veiled continuation of coloniality in education. Finally, the chapter discusses how the relationship between conditionality and coloniality can affect epistemic democracy, leading to the conclusion that the link between them prevents epistemic democracy from being officially constructed as a determinant of teaching excellence.

In order to be able to deconstruct how coloniality in education has come about, a critical look at the origins of colonialism as a broader phenomenon affecting societies is required. Most analyses agree that postcolonial authors such as Walter Mignolo or Gayatri Spivak have laid key scholarly groundwork underlying the current understandings of the ways in which academic institutions and groups of individuals associated with the West, First World countries, European Enlightenment and modernity (understood not as the modern world-system but rather as being associated with the universality of modern and Western-centric

© The Author(s) 2019

49

A. Hayes, *Inclusion, Epistemic Democracy and International Students*,
https://doi.org/10.1007/978-3-030-11401-5_3

50   A. Hayes

knowledge) have grown their prestige at the expense of silencing other knowledges.

As Mignolo (2002) explains, the eighteenth century was dominated by two distinctive shifts. Firstly, the political and economic power was beginning to be shifted from the South to the North of the globe and secondly, Europe was heavily focused on nation-building. Mignolo (2002) argues that when some European countries (such as Britain, France and Germany) mutually reinforced nation-building, it was through colonial expansion. Despite colonialism (in the sense of taking political control of knowledge production and exercising intellectual superiority) not initially being the primary concern of countries such as England and France, especially in America where the interests were mainly commercial (Mignolo 2002), England specifically had civilising missions elsewhere. For instance, Williams (1984) argues that the expansion of English education to other nations such as India in the nineteenth century was based on the idea of 'enlightenment'. This idea legitimised the process of mandating British education in former colonies, one which also enabled colonial governments to institutionalise the superiority of the English education system, simultaneously giving them a mandate to exclude those who benefited from it from equal treatment (Williams 1984).

Tamson Pietsch (2012) analysed this imperial expansion of knowledge as being reflected in approaches to internationalisation in the UK today. She posits that the colonial versions of university internationalisation, which, *inter alia*, mandated British education in some of the former colonies, have much to tell about the perils of internationalisation nowadays. Pietsch (2012, p. i) argues that 'sanctioning ways of knowing was a means of acquiring dominion over both land and people', concluding that:

> University internationalisation in the 19th and early 20th centuries was a highly unequal and contingent phenomenon. It was about imperial rule as well as education, exclusion as well as access, and it created discontentment as well as satisfaction. In this, it bears strong similarities to internationalisation today. If the UK higher education sector is to develop a critical understanding of its international entanglements, it needs to pay

close attention to this earlier university world. It helped to establish the uneven lines of global connection that, in the field of higher education as elsewhere, remain with us to this day. (Pietsch 2012, p. ii)

The 'uneven lines of global connection' and their relationship to colonialism have also been critiqued by Mignolo (2002) as being responsible for the generally accepted notion of modernity—i.e. that the West was the house of epistemology. This notion was driven by the premise that 'Western expansion was not only economic and political but also educational and intellectual because in essence, the geopolitics of knowledge is organized around the diversification, through history, of the colonial and the imperial differences' (Mignolo 2002, p. 59). In addition, the expansion of Western capitalism seems to have also contributed to the perception of the West as the 'house' of epistemology because as Wallerstein (1997) argued, domestic ideology of Western cultures of scholarship that spread with capitalism was assumed to have universal scope, valid for all times and people. This meant that the desire for expansion that came with capitalism eliminated the idea that alternative knowledge, produced outside of the Western civilisation, could also be valid (ibid.).

Thus, modernity, in the sense of the historical development of knowledge, as well as Western capitalism, emphasise Western Europe as universal. What this meant in the eighteenth and nineteenth centuries, and in many instance also occupying today's thinking, is that 'there can be no others' in the education system, inscribing 'conceptualization of knowledge to a geopolitical space (Western Europe) and eras[-ing] the possibility of even thinking about a conceptualization and distribution of knowledge emanating from other local histories (China, India, Islam, etc.)' (Mignolo 2002, p. 59). From this perspective, the colonised parts of the world were, and still can be, seen as unable to produce any intellectual outcomes because the hierarchies instilled by imperialism disqualify colonised nations from being capable of producing anything else than primitive objects (Mignolo 2009). Such epistemic violence towards the colonised nations has also translated into the context of education, giving rise to a phenomenon known as coloniality.

Coloniality, Conditionality and Higher Education

Aníbal Quijano (2000) was one of the key scholars who developed the concept of coloniality as a specific type of power that created and maintained hierarchical relationships between those who were historically conquering and the conquered. These relationships were built around the idea of world capitalism that, as a specific and new social relation based on domination, was the axis around which the new pattern of power was articulated (Quijano 2000). Naturally, as Quijano (2000) argued, when there is domination, there will also be the 'superiors' and the 'inferiors' and by extension, their associated cultural and intellectual differences will also be coded as such.

Developing the ideas of domination and segregation into 'superiors' and 'inferiors' in the context of education, postcolonial scholars generally agree that coloniality continues to enable uneven power relations in the classroom that subsidise Western influence (Kapoor 2008; Stein et al. 2016; Silva 2015). Coloniality in education has been broadly accepted to mean the logic of cultural, social, political and intellectual domination over foreign students in an education system, leading to the presumption of a single path of human progress and of the universal value of Western knowledge (Stein et al. 2016). Alternative perspectives of knowledge and modes of learning are viewed as 'inferior' and behind the West in time; hence, as explained in Chapter 2, the persistent education discourses about the need for 'upskilling' international students through conditionality. Such conditionality, as Silva (2015) argues, reinforces representations of the West as superior and international students as lacking moral and intellectual capacity (Silva 2015). It therefore 'limits the questions that can be asked and the answers that can be provided, which often leads to the normalisation of existing social hierarchies and assumptions, and the delegitimisation or erasure of other imaginaries and possibilities' (Stein et al. 2016, p. 4).

Coloniality, being an aspect of modern/colonial global imaginary, can be said to function as an invisible frame that structures meaning and understanding which determine which and whose perspectives are credible (Taylor 2004). The key meanings coloniality has shaped at

3 Conditionality as a Veiled Continuation ... 53

universities is that the universality of Western knowledge can only be sustained in contrast to the partiality of non-Wester knowledge, which, in consequence, leads to the following situations:

> Today higher education institutions continue to reproduce an epistemological hierarchy wherein Western knowledges are presumed to be universally relevant and valuable, while non-Western knowledges are either patronisingly celebrated as 'local culture', commodified or appropriated for Western gain, or else, not recognised as knowledge at al'. (Stein and Andreotti 2016, p. 2)

Spivak (1988) calls this process 'epistemic violence', Aman (2018) refers to it as 'epistemological privilege'. But, terminology aside, what this primarily means is that there is a meta-narrative that functions as an ideology positioning that there is a linear educational success of the 'other'. Coloniality therefore makes the 'other' navigate the colonialist dynamics as, in this way, the 'other' can work towards their success in a linear and organised way, which is simultaneously positioned to be the only way of correctly learning knowledge. The aim of this book is to propose a system that can rupture this ideology and mandate universities to engage with the complexities of knowledge production that this rupture can cause.

For this reason, it is not enough to consider coloniality from the perspective of 'cultural difference' because, as explained by Mignolo (2005, p. 37), 'the notion of cultural differences overlooks the relation of power, while the concept of "colonial difference" [which could be understood as the space in which coloniality is enacted] is based precisely on imperial/colonial power differentials'. It is thought that the changes to the TEF metrics proposed in this book target exactly the type of colonial difference described here. They do not target the 'cultural difference' because they go beyond the notions of bridging the gap between the cultures through curricular shifts or global festivals and activities organised by universities with the view to culturally connect. Yes, it is true that efforts to culturally connect may include the language of 'other', exposure to their 'otherness' and the accumulation of facts about their culture but, as Perry and Southwell (2011) suggest, these are only the means towards a particular type of comprehension of knowledge but teach people nothing about the power relations that 'other' this knowledge. People can therefore understand the knowledge and culture of others (and thus be referred to as being 'interculturally connected') but they may at the same time continue to exercise epistemological violence over those who are 'culturally different', through expectations towards them to adapt. And as mentioned in the preface to this book, the intention here is not to challenge the value of shifts and activities to culturally connect, but rather to show that, on their own, they are not sufficient because they do not address the issue of power that is enacted through coloniality. The proposed changes to the TEF rankings in this book, on the other hand, target this power by assessing universities on their ability to recognise subjectivities of international and home students' knowledge as equal and on representing one another in ways that do not point to the influence of political, social, economic and educational dominance.

By extension, the proposed rankings provide a critical response and a practical solution to key questions about coloniality in education. The first one of these questions is about whether it will ever be possible for universities, being mainly supported by the nation-states, to enact and action any actual eradication of coloniality? The responses from recent literature to this question suggest that eradicating coloniality would work if there was a deliberate and sustained supplementation of Western curricula with non-Western perspectives (for review of this proposition see Stein and Andreotti 2016). The book however additionally proposes, drawing on work by scholars such as Gorski (2008), that good intentions to organise such supplementation are not enough because, on their own, these curricular shifts will not work as they do not have the backing from the political power. And they do not have the backing from the political power because 'the boundaries of the institution and of acceptable modes of knowledge production and critique are still firmly policed by white [Western-centric] and capitalist power structures' (Stein and Andreotti 2016, p. iii). Also, often political power does not support the supplementation of Western curricula with non-Western ones because requests to decolonise the curriculum are often dismissed as ungrateful and as trying to challenge the credibility and international prestige of the knowledge from a nation state (e.g. Fallis 2011). What happens instead is that foreigners who arrive to study in a host country nation state are expected to be grateful to have been given access to this knowledge, where expression of opinions at variance with those officially held in the curriculum could be perceived as uncivil and barbaric. Universities already do a lot, as the official line goes, to diversify higher education, as they encourage international students recruitment and their contribution to universities (The Higher Education Commission 2018). But their contribution is welcomed only insofar it does not challenge existing measures of achievement, for example, in terms of teaching excellence or existing power relations, because, as Chapter 5 analyses in detail, encouraging knowledge contributions from beyond the boundaries of the nation state does not count as an official referent of teaching excellence. Instead, what counts is how much international students can adapt to perform well in the national education system and how much they pay into the national system.

It is argued in this book that presently, the TEF represents high levels of conditionality when it comes to inclusion of international students. The key problem here is that this conditionality is accepted and legitimised in the TEF, as well as in other public policy discourses reviewed in Chapter 2, which clearly give out one message—that international students' success is premised on the degree of difference in reference to the universal standard. Such messages securely place conditionality in the public idea and encourage publicly accepted thinking that it is OK to be superior because through conditionality, 'we' are helping 'them' to overcome their disadvantage. Due to the fact that inclusion is conceptualised as conditional, because that is what is needed for others to 'help them out', it consequently becomes a veiled continuation of coloniality; one that is not officially recognised as a problem. Instead, it is represented as something charitable and as a benevolent action, to the extent that foreign students are expected to be grateful and refrain from any dissent.

Positioning this conditionality as a benevolent act also means that it becomes additionally amplified at times of crisis—then it is almost always double-emphasised as a 'good thing' for international students. At times of crisis, the official discourse that universities are proud to welcome international students is especially overamplified and additional efforts are made to get this message out in the media and any other outlets that may reach international students. When there is a crisis, such as Brexit for instance or the changing trends in international students mobility which threaten the position of the UK as one of the top destination countries, universities (wrongly!) seem to think it is a good idea to highlight that *they* will be responsible for international students' success. And whilst in some cases the intention behind this may be good, it automatically sends a message that there is 'us' and 'them' and that the success of the latter depends on the conditions set by the former. Such conditioning can already be seen in the TEF, through 'declarations of help', including statements such as 'England's world-class higher education system is open to anyone with the potential to benefit from it' (BIS 2015, p. 36) which is why 'students receive effective support in order to achieve their educational goals and potential' (BIS 2015, p. 33). The TEF is also explicit that this support is offered because the UK may potentially be facing international students' recruitment crisis, which is why propositions to support international students are included in the TEF to 'safeguard the strong international reputation for English providers' (BIS 2015, p. 57) and because 'information about the quality of teaching [provided through the TEF] is vital to UK productivity' (ibid., p. 19) and *not* because the UK suddenly realised that they need to end coloniality in education. Dismissal of the presence of coloniality in education, however, results in what Andreotti (2007) refers to as 'sanctioned ignorance' (constitutive disavowal) of the role of conditionality in the creation of a situation whereby the nations of the First world (i.e. Western Europe) lead the rest of the world and justify project of development of the 'Other' as a civilising mission. This kind of thinking legitimises a denial, individual and institutional, that there could ever be a different 'project' with regards to international students, one that is based on inclusion enacted through epistemic democracy.

For Andreotti (2007), the epistemic violence that is allowed through sanctioned ignorance works both ways because the Third World wants to be civilised and catch up with the West. Perhaps that is why, as noted by Marginson (2015, p. 8), international students still arrive in Britain because they 'want to acquire a UK education in its own often traditional terms'. This may be resulting in situations whereby international students may feel they cannot carry authority or meaning for the host institutions without acquiring the knowledge that is given to them, which may simultaneously instill in them the idea that they are subordinates.

Spivak is critical of the way Western institutions produce knowledge about the Third World as it results in increased epistemological privilege of the Western knower. Some of the international students interviewed as part of the research on which this book is based were also critical about this privilege and ways in which the assumed universality of Western knowledge represents the 'other'. For example, one student said:

> if they [UK universities] generalise, they need to do the kind of generalisation which doesn't insult the other culture or which doesn't look down on other cultures, and at the same time, it makes people aware that different kind of things [i.e. alternative knowledges] can also be there (Education Student, England)

But in the meantime, as explained by Kapoor (2008), the privilege of the Western knower makes that knower:

> Liable to speak *for* the subaltern, justifying power and domination, naturalising Western superiority, essentialising ethnicity, or asserting ethnocultural or class identity, all in the name of the subaltern. In so doing, it is liable to do harm to the subaltern. (Kapoor 2008, p. 45)

That is perhaps why, due to the assumed liability of the Western knower to speak for the subaltern, Marginson (2015, p. 8), when analysing specifically the context of the UK, notes that universities need to be sensitive to the fact that international students do not come to England, as adults, to make themselves into the clones of the English and to be more English than the English. He explains that most international students nurture their founding identity along with their new identity and interpret the UK curriculum through the lens of their own prior intellectual formation. Thus, the purpose behind proposing the new TEF metrics in this book is to mandate teaching at universities that respects this prior intellectual formation because, as Marginson (2015, p. 8) notes, the UK 'are not the last word or the gold standard, despite what [their] marketing says; and local students have much to gain by learning from international students. But we [the British] are not yet good at persuading local students to open their minds to international students'. This is because, as he explains, British universities are influenced by cultural inertia and commercial imperatives.

It is argued here that the proposed changes to the TEF could at least be one of the many steps that need to be taken towards changing the cultural inertia and the commercial imperatives. Yes, these changes would still function as a commercial ranking (see Chapters 4 and 5 in the book) but the nature and scope of this ranking would change. And that is what is important. It is thought that the ranking proposed in this book would be one representing key principles behind the movement known as 'interculturalidad' (Aman 2018)—i.e. one that will hold universities to account to create, through relevant pedagogies, spaces for voices that come from the undersite of the colonial difference.

'Interculturalidad', which translates as 'interculturality', emerged in tandem with the increasing presence of Indigenous people in politics. It is claimed that the election of Evo Morales, the first indigenous president of Bolivia, signified the political importance of interculturalidad as an official step towards ending colonialization (Walsh 2009, cited in Aman 2018). In its broad sense, interculturalidad is used to describe actions towards reclaiming the identity of indigenous people and revaluing their culture. The term is said to have come into being when the indigenous people found themselves oppressed because of the social struggles they were experiencing due to class and race divisions, as well as the capitalist reality (Aman 2018). Aman (2018, p. 63) however contends that interculturalidad should not be mistaken for interculturality (as its direct translation suggests) because interculturality, in most European and meta-national discourses, is used as a 'method of facing the cultural challenges of every multicultural society by uniting around *universally shared values* emerging from the interplay of these cultural specificities'. The focus on universality therefore represents more the colonial echoes as opposed to the key principles of interculturalidad because the latter 'is intertwined with the act of restorative justice for the way in which the nation state for centuries has turned its indigenous populations into its blind spot, with a particular focus on epistemic change' (Aman 2018, p. 63). The intention of the proposed changes to the TEF metric is also to start epistemic change, especially in the sense of ending the dismissal of intellectual capital of international students and their knowledges as non-empirical and invalid. It is thought therefore that these changes reflect many of the underlying principles of interculturalidad, and it would be rather inadequate to associate them with interculturality which, through the emphasis on universality of (Western) knowledge as a factor that can connect cultures, simultaneously risks disconnecting specific (non-Western) knowledges from any opportunities for them of being given a status of being scientific and true.

Thus, rather than being associated with interculturality, the proposed changes to the TEF in this book should be seen as an attempt to decolonise higher education, especially in the sense of ending educational coloniality. And whilst there are many meanings of decolonisation of higher education which are contested and at times at odds with one another (for a useful typology see Andreotti et al. 2015), the meaning of decolonisation that the proposed changes in this book particularly reflect is one that is based on:

> efforts to resist distinct but intertwined processes of colonisation, to enact transformation and redress in reference to the historical and ongoing effects of these processes, and to create and keep alive modes of knowing, being, and relating that these processes seek to eradicate. Colonisation (…) [has] both material and epistemic dimensions, which together shape social relations and enshrine categories that are then used to justify: (…) claims about the universality of modern Western reason, objectification and exploitation of 'nature', capitalist property relations and modes of production [and] possessive individualism. (Stein and Andreotti 2016, p. i)

Thus, through challenging the universality of the Western knowledge in university classrooms and encouraging epistemic dimensions of knowing that this universality seeks to eradicate, the proposed rankings in this book should be seen as attempting to reconstruct epistemic norms in university classrooms. They stand against colonisation of knowledge and detaching it from its local histories. To detach knowledge from its local histories would be impossible, because then, we would effectively be suggesting that it is possible to produce knowledge that is neutral and not context-specific. This is a false premise on which colonisation of education has in fact been built, through placing a lot of emphasis on universality. Instead, what the proposed metrics in this book intend to do is to create classroom situations whereby no epistemology becomes dominant or is universalised as, through the assessments of pedagogy that are captured under these metrics (see Chapters 6 and 7), these metrics will keep each epistemology rooted in the intellectual traditions of all people who attend that class. By focusing on the reciprocity between these epistemologies, these metrics will additionally ensure that all epistemologies are equalised.

The proposed rankings also stand against material dimensions of colonialism and coloniality in education which, as explained above, have legitimised conditionality of equality for international students through the influence of the present shape and nature of the commercial university rankings. Thus, through proposing a new ranking, the book should be seen as also being linked to material attempts to decolonise higher education as the scope of the outcomes that are assessed through this new ranking is thought to shape new social relations that can potentially end the colonial categorisations of people. And if these rankings are in operation, there should no longer be any justification for conditionality.

The need for the new TEF ranking is based on the premise that epistemological silencing takes place not only because of the historicised influence of imperialism and world divisions into First and Third world, but also because preventing epistemological silencing is not 'measured' in any official rankings. This idea offers a useful conceptual extension, in addition to some of the historicised approaches to decolonisation of education. The book posits that historicised critiques attempting to explain why epistemological silencing takes place are not sufficient because silencing of some epistemologies is also related to the influence of commercial rankings, whose governance is global, which shapes specific property relations, power and modes of knowledge production that are established above and often in complete exteriority to the boundaries and histories of individual nation states. This last point could be seen as being supported by the findings from the German case presented in Chapter 2, which suggests that it is not that important any more where production of knowledge takes place; what seems to matter more is which products of the histories of some nation states have remained to be associated with the European enlightenment and with the spread of capitalism, as well as what their joint influence on the present levels of marketisation of education is. There are obvious ways in which university rankings and their associated prestige and misconceptions of internationalisation (see the Introduction to this book) can be seen as being exactly those products. And whilst it could be argued that decolonisation of higher education should attempt to eradicate rankings overall, it is instead posited here, based on the view that university rankings will not go away (Hazelkorn 2015), that a more realistic solution to ending coloniality in education can be achieved through the proposed changes to university rankings offered in this book.

The proposition and the nature of the rankings presented in this book are based on the conceptual premise that it is not so much the histories of countries, although they are important, but rather these countries' commercial and capitalist needs in education that prevent epistemologically diverse knowledge production. Yes, these capitalist needs are Western-centric, the book does not dispute this link. The main proposition in the book however is that, as the capitalist needs are likely to continue to influence universities, we need to have capitalist tools that will equalise non-Western knowledges with Western ones. What the proposed metrics will *not* do is to take universities out of the nation-state and to reduce nations' capitalist needs. They can however de-politicise university rankings through challenging the current nature of the reaches of global capitalism and ways in which the capitalist needs of individual countries are met. It is thought the proposed rankings can do so through putting forward a plan to measure the education process that is ongoing and does not represent a distinct set of benchmarks that 'certify' only Western knowledge as scientific, truthful or universal, and through that, disqualify 'others' from being intellectually equal. Instead the education process that will be measured in these new rankings will seek to acknowledge all students as equally qualified knowers. Consequently, the new TEF rankings have a potential to develop a new understanding of teaching excellence—one which is constitutive of epistemic democracy as one of its key determinants.

Teaching Excellence Understood as Epistemic Democracy

Broadly, epistemic democracy can be taken to mean equivalence of different geopolitical sources of knowledge (Mignolo 2009, 2011). In the context of this book, epistemic democracy specifically refers to the pedagogical process that actively strives to acknowledge these sources as equally valid, by promoting the idea of all 'knowers' in the classroom as being equal. Epistemic democracy in this book, especially if it is to be associated with teaching excellence, therefore denotes classroom activism towards ending subordination of those who have been described as non-people, inferiors, primitives and barbarians (Mignolo 2009, 2011). It rests around the idea of inter-epistemic dialogue—that is, interactions that emphasise the difference between participants as sources of critical knowledge 'by making visible co-existing paradigms of thought that have been silenced and disavowed' (Aman 2018, p. 89).

Epistemic democracy as a determinant of teaching excellence therefore stands up to coloniality which, as explained in the previous section of this chapter, is based on the logic of cultural and intellectual domination over foreign students in an education system. Being a determinant of teaching excellence, epistemic democracy would instead aim to target those aspects of teaching and learning that have historically hidden, silenced and forced themselves upon learners that have been positioned as less globally relevant. Using epistemic democracy as a determinant of teaching excellence would therefore mean getting universities to arrive at the point whereby they actively, routinely and officially practise 'universal participation on terms of equality of all inquirers' (Anderson 2012, p. 172). But universal here does *not* mean common—in the sense

3 Conditionality as a Veiled Continuation ...

that the knowledge contributed by inquirers should be general and 'all-round', i.e. being able to be applied across borders and all knowers in the same way. Universal here means related to and being done by all people without fear from coercion and discrimination, so they can all universally contribute their intellectual capital. The understanding of epistemic democracy aimed to be promoted by the TEF metrics discussed in this book rejects the assumption that rational and universal truth are independent of whoever presents them, to whom and why (Mignolo 2011). The proposed metrics strongly contest the common knowledge idea to inclusion of international students which some of the intercultural approaches advocate. Nor do they propose to measure any such common knowledge. Instead, the proposed metrics aim to give greater prominence to the difference in how knowledge is constructed, by whom and how students' developmental interests can be served by constructing knowledge in those different ways. So the type of epistemic democracy that is sought through the proposed TEF metrics is not about replacing the Eurocentric domination of knowledge with the socially situated epistemologies of the knowledge produced by the 'other'. Rather, it is an attempt to develop determinants of teaching excellence that offer a form of educational inquiry in the classroom that can destabilise the current knowledge production system presently excluding and devaluing 'others'.

Proposing that epistemic democracy is a determinant of teaching excellence, and showing in this book how it could be initiated by and work in practice via adequate TEF metrics, should therefore be seen as an attempt to achieve a transformation from a *uni*-veristy to *pluri*-versity (Boidin et al. 2012). This would mean acknowledging 'others' as thinking and knowledge producing subjects, which, by extension, would be a sign of 'pluriversalism'—that is a fundamental re-founding of our ways of thinking to create universities that promote a different understanding of universality from that enshrined by colonialism. This new understanding would mean searching 'for universal knowledge as pluriversal knowledge (…) through horizontal dialogues among different traditions of thought' (Boidin et al. 2012, p. 2). It would require the 'construction of "pluriverses" of meaning by taking seriously the knowledge production of non-Western traditions and genealogies of thought' (ibid., p. 2).

Making epistemic democracy to be a determinant of teaching excellence does not therefore represent 'harm-reduction' strategies. On the contrary, this proposition targets the causes not the symptoms of the epistemological silencing that currently structures intellectual relationships within universities. It therefore has a future potential to prevent the limits of the current definitions of teaching excellence, which do not target the premise shaping the idea that educational equality of people like international students is dependent on modernity and colonial opportunities.

There are of course many understandings of teaching excellence in higher education (see for example, Dunkin 1995; Skelton et al. 2005; Gregory and Gregory 2013), so more are also critiqued in Chapter 4. However, the latest review of key conceptualisations of this notion (Gunn and Fisk 2013), as well as conceptualisations of teaching excellence evoked by the TEF and its sister equivalents around the world (also presented in Chapter 4) suggest that teaching excellence has not yet been considered from the perspective of democratising knowledge production in the classroom. This gap makes this book ever so important. To date, the key 'problems' with teaching excellence have been concluded to be related to the lack of articulation around the differences between threshold quality and teaching excellence (this is also deconstructed in Chapter 4), the lack of sophistication in conceptualisation of university teaching excellence, particularly in terms of changing expectations of academics, the lack of representatively diverse conceptualisations of teaching excellence (given the diversity of the sector), that there is little distinction between teaching excellence in teaching-oriented and research-oriented institutions and that there is a gap between teaching excellence practice and educational theory (Gunn and Fisk 2013). Such findings raise a number of areas which the proposition in this book to include epistemic democracy as a referent of teaching excellence addresses.

Firstly, the changing expectations of academics mean that they are sometimes expected to teach the content of their subject-disciplines but they may also sometimes be made responsible through their teaching for the broader socialisation of students into a democratic society and the knowledge economy. What is significant is that, as noted by Gunn and Fisk (2013), ways in which academics identify with these demands is how their orientations towards teaching and definitions of teaching excellence will be shaped. So, for instance, if academics support the premise of conditional equality discussed in the first section of this chapter, or if they fall in step with policy representations of international students as economic objects and beneficiaries of the prestigious English education system (reviewed in Chapter 2), their conceptualisations of teaching excellence are unlikely to be based around principles of epistemic democracy. Similarly, if despite the increased diversity of students around the world, universities in most countries do not conceptualise excellent teaching as giving all students the status of equally qualified knowers and instead, problematise excellent teaching with respect to diversity as being mostly about 'upskilling' students from different socio-economic and cultural backgrounds, they arguably reinforce the same colonial lines which position these students as 'inferior' and needing the help of their 'superiors'. If there is no greater emphasis on diversification of epistemologies of knowledge at research-active universities, which arguably are responsible for the majority of knowledge production, how can those teachers consider themselves to be excellent when they might be running a risk of shaping a knowledge production system that is Eurocentric and influenced by the limits of the colonial universality? Finally, if there is no link between teaching practice and educational theory, for which there is a need and which, according to Gunn and Fisk (2013), could be addressed by models conceptualising teaching excellence that are large-scale and targeted at the whole system (i.e. such as the one discussed in Section III of this book, rather than personalised efforts operationalised by individuals), we will continue to receive small scale proposals (so called 'teaching innovations') that, at best, can only probably reduce some effects of the damage that has already been done. The proposed TEF changes in this book, on the other hand, do not represent such 'harm-reduction' techniques. They do not target harm that has already been done but rather aim to *prevent* harm because they target systemic changes that make the system harmful to international students in the first place. Through creating rankings that focus on the educational processes of reciprocity and pedagogies leading to equivalence of all knowledges, the proposed changes to the TEF help resolve the double binds of conflicting objectives to, on the one hand, decolonise universities but on the other, to fulfil the obligation to compete in national and international assessments of teaching excellence that harm international (and home) students alike. Through addressing these double binds, the proposed TEF rankings also make an important theoretical contribution by extending our understanding of the existing notions of educational equality.

Stuart Tannock (2018) has recently reviewed the notion of educational equality with reference to international students, drawing on five interpretations of educational equality developed by Jencks (1988, cited in Tannock 2018). Tannock (2018) attempted to deconstruct how nationally defined concepts, policies and practices surrounding equality in education should be re-defined in the context of higher education that is becoming increasingly internationalised. The standpoint of this book is that, as the first step, they should include students' rights to epistemic democracy.

In his review of education equality, Tannock (2018) returned to its relationship to the nation state. He highlighted that, although, in principle, all potential students should have the same access and prospects for educational achievement, these are often influenced by people's national and social backgrounds. Marginson (2012) had already deconstructed this influence in relation to international students specifically and pointed out that despite the declared freedom of every person to exercise social, cultural, legal and economic rights in the country of education, international students are not able to exercise these rights because they are governed by different regulatory frameworks than the home students. These differing rules increase the likelihood of international students being subject to coercion, and in some instances even enable and legitimise discrimination (ibid.). For instance, the very issue of international students' fees reflects this type of educational inequality because international students pay substantially higher amounts of money for the same benefits home students can access for a lot less. Different regulatory regimes also mean that, for instance, in cases where international students are made to work over-time and for less money than home students, they are unlikely to make official complaints about their situation as if they do, they will have to reveal breaching employment rules regarding the number of hours they are allowed to work under their visas, and as a result, they will lose an important source of income (e.g. Marginson 2012). Experiences of finding accommodation in a private rental market are another example where differing conditions to demonstrate international students' eligibility to rent in the country of education have been used to discriminate against them and affected their security (e.g. Deumert et al. 2005; Forbes-Mewett and Nyland 2008). Those differing rules and regulations therefore de-power international students as the lack of the same privilege as home students and the same social capital makes it more difficult for them to exercise equality in education (e.g. Calder et al. 2016).

Tannock's (2018) review shows that key scholars have been exploring ideas of educational equality related mostly to notions of 'equality of opportunity', 'equal outcomes in educational achievement' and 'educational adequacy' (meaning that there should be some absolute level of educational achievement that every member of society reaches). This brings to attention the fact that notions of educational equality as epistemic democracy have not yet received much attention. There are however some authors cited in Tannock's (2018) review who could be seen to potentially begin to lay some groundwork for thinking about educational equality in terms of epistemic democracy that this book is trying to prompt. These authors explore the notion of 'equality of condition' which is argued here is relevant for the type of educational equality that the book would like to be associated with epistemic democracy. 'Equality of condition' promotes an understanding of educational equality as a matter of relational justice, concerned not only with distributive justice (i.e. whether students have equal access to educational opportunities, resources and outcomes), but mainly with 'how educational institutions can help students learn to be equal, by initiating them into the practices and habits of relating to one another as equals' (Laden 2013, cited in Tannock 2018, p. 18). Tannock (2018) draws here in particular on the work of Kathleen Lynch and John Baker (2005, p. 132) who propose that 'resources; respect and recognition; love; care and solidarity; power; and working and learning' are the founding principles for creating an equality of condition. He summarises its founding principles in the following way:

> Educational equality [on the account of equality of condition] thus concerns everything from the distribution of resources within an educational system, to recruitment and admissions procedures, to the design of the curriculum, pedagogy and assessment practices, to the nature of staff-student and student-student relationships, to the promotion of student voice and democratic decision-making within schools, colleges and universities. (Tannock 2018, p. 18)

Thus, equality of condition is in many ways akin to the notions of epistemic democracy that drive the development of the TEF metric proposed in this book. Both, equality of condition and epistemic democracy seem to be based on the idea that, firstly, students should have an equal chance to contribute subjective knowledge based on the epistemology of their own origin, without fear from discrimination and prejudice and secondly, for this knowledge to be made equivalent with the perspectives established by the nation state. Equality of condition therefore counterindicates the type conditionality which, as explained above, currently prevents the lack of this equivalence to be problematized. It has been argued elsewhere that epistemic quivalence is currently denied to some students, especially those who are the 'other' because of the existence of two types of phenomena that lead to epistemic injustice (Fricker 2007). These phenomena have been conceived by Miranda Fricker (2007) to include 'testimonial injustice' and 'hermeneutical injustice'. The former denotes a situation when the speaker's credibility is challenged because the hearer is prejudiced towards them (because of their origin, ethnicity, sexuality, etc.) and the latter is based on the assumption that this particular speaker cannot make sense of what they are experiencing, or learning, because their culture did not offer them opportunities to critically engage with these experiences (Fricker 2007). Through the occurrence of these two phenomena, speakers can therefore be challenged as qualified 'knowers' because, by not being given credibility, their ability to contribute knowledge is limited.

The proposed metrics in this book are, on the other hand, thought to help reduce the effects of testimonial and hermeneutic injustice, if not entirely eradicate them, as the time passes, and we get used to the idea and are obligated to think about it by our teaching excellence assessments, that perspectives beyond the spaces of colonial difference are not inferior. Through the measurement outcomes in these metrics which emphasise that knowledge in the classroom is co-produced by all knowers, the metrics are believed to dispute the supremacy of knowledge produced in certain geopolitical borders and therefore eliminate the influences stemming from 'hermeneutical injustice' which pre-supposes lower levels of understandings of knowledge by certain students. If the proposed metrics ever function as official rankings, these pre-suppositions will simply no longer be legitimate. 'Testimonial injustice' is also believed to be potentially eradicated by the proposed metric because, by finally being given access to intellectual benefits arising from internationalisation, home students and their institutions will begin to appreciate that their own knowledges are poorer, in intellect and content, when the knowledges of other speakers are discredited based on outdated prejudices and modernity. They would then be expected to stop the process of dishonouring 'others' as credible knowers and should soon uncover a new system of knowing and reason which reflect cosmopolitanism, *not* coloniality.

But for this new system of knowing to be uncovered, it is imperative that epistemic democracy, in the sense described at the start of this section, becomes an official referent of teaching excellence. Why? Because only when it is, epistemic democracy and its associated referents proposed in this book have a potential to start what Andreotti et al. (2015) call a 'radical-reform'. Radical-reform recognises epistemological dominance and its relationships to systems (such as the TEF exercise) which 'highlight the historical, discursive and affective dynamics that ground hegemonic and ethnocentric practices' (Andreotti et al. 2015, p. 26). From this perspective, epistemological dominance is recognised as a systemic problem. It is therefore different to individual efforts to culturally connect (via curricular shifts or global festivals at universities showcasing cultures and food from international students' countries) which do not demand a 'more drastic interruption of business-as-usual' (p. 26).

This type of radical reform should not however be seen as an attempt to 'fix' the system because the proposed TEF changes do not intend to make the system work *more* for the oppressed (i.e. international students). If that were the case, the proposed metrics could ultimately lead to further reinforcing the superior position of the oppressor (i.e. home students) by suggesting that they have a responsibility to end the discrimination of international students by using their power and privilege to 'fix' them. Instead, the proposed metrics intend to create alternatives to situations whereby the oppressors take responsibility for freeing the oppressed by transforming the ways, through adequate teaching, which currently enable those already in power to gain more power. These ways reflect thinking that including those who are different should be managed on the terms of those who are doing the including. The radical reform initiated by the changes to the TEF metrics, on the other hand, proposes that an equal space for the difference should be created; a space to which those who are doing the including should come but not with intentions to fix but rather to embrace and reciprocate. By their very nature, intentions to reciprocate reject the idea that a mere addition of other ways of knowing (which may be taking place through, for instance, misunderstandings of the internationalisation of the curriculum) will ultimately change the system that encourages epistemological violence. As Andreotti et al. (2015, p. 27) explain, 'the incorporation of multiple ways of knowing (grafted onto the same hegemonic ontological foundation that is left unexamined—[e.g. such as the TEF]) through strategies of equity, access, voice, recognition, representation or re-distribution', does not change anything. What is needed is a system that does not assume that there is one ontological position which is dominant; rather, the system needs to show that alternative ways of knowing are developed in spaces that are external to that ontological position and it needs to teach people that these ways of knowing are equally valid.

Finally, what makes the kind of thinking that such a system may potentially be developed by the proposed TEF metrics legitimate is the notion that many people may be afraid of or reluctant to create this system *unless* it functions as a university ranking. Otherwise, by engaging with this system, they would potentially be subjecting themselves to a loss of privilege. They would also need to think about outweighing the commercial benefits that compliance with epistemological violence currently brings about (whilst allowing them to be seen as doing good) vs. the moral and ethical disenchantment with epistemological hegemony that currently brings no such benefits. The book outlines in the next chapter, through the review of the commercial power of university rankings, why universities may deny the existence of epistemological violence and continue to support it, despite knowing it is wrong. But what the review of university rankings in the next chapter simultaneously brings to mind is the notion that if the same people were to disenchant themselves from this denial, they would need something else, another system, to look for certainty and directionality of their strategies, in the same way that the current rankings guarantee them. They therefore need another ranking. People and universities may be afraid of leaving the system that currently guarantees their prestige and creates perceptions that they are doing something good, even though, deep down, they know the system is wrong. So they need another ranking that offers them a tangible exit from the complicity with epistemological violence that the current rankings lock them in. It is argued here that they can be provided with the option of such an exit through the type of university ranking that will measure pedagogies that discourage selectivity in validating only certain types of knowledge and encourage openness and recognition of all types of knowledges, without any conditionality. So if such critical pedagogy is to be the centre of this new ranking, it makes sense to propose that this ranking is part of the national and international assessments of teaching excellence, such as the TEF. This ranking could focus attention on the educational process of *relationality* between unconditional inclusion of alternative ways of knowing and teaching practices that are used to shape such inclusion. This would however require, as indicated above, new referents of teaching excellence, i.e. ones that problematise it as a process supporting epistemic democracy. These referents are outlined in Section III of the book.

References

Aman, R. (2018). *Decolonising intercultural education: Colonial differences, the geopolitics of knowledge, and inter-epistemic dialogue.* London: Routledge.

Anderson, E. (2012). Epistemic justice as a virtue of social institutions. *Social Epistemology, 26*(2), 163–173.

Andreotti, V. (2007). An ethical engagement with the other: Spivak's ideas on education. *Critical Literacy: Theories and Practices, 1*(1), 69–79.

Andreotti, V., Stein, S., Ahenakew, C., & Hunt, D. (2015). Mapping interpretations of decolonization in the context of higher education. *Decolonization: Indigeneity, Education & Society, 4*(1), 21–40.

BIS (Department for Business, Innovation and Skills). (2015). *Fullfilling our potential: Teaching excellence, social mobility and student choice.* Green Paper, cm 9141, HMG, UK.

Boidin, C., Cohen, J., & Grosfoguel, R. (2012). Introduction: From university to pluriversity: A decolonial approach to the present crisis of western universities. *Human Architecture: Journal of the Sociology of Self-Knowledge, 10*(1), 1–6.

Calder, M. M., Richter, S., Mao, Y., Kovacs Burns, K., Mogale, R. S., & Danko, M. (2016). International students attending Canadian universities: Their experiences with housing, finances, and other issues. *Canadian Journal of Higher Education, 46*(2), 92–110.

Deumert, A., Marginson, S., Nyland, C., Ramia, G., & Sawir, E. (2005). The social and economic security of cross-border students in Australia. *Global Social Policy, 5,* 329–352.

Dunkin, M. J. (1995). Concepts of teaching and teaching excellence in higher education. *Higher Education Research and Development, 14*(1), 21–33.

Fallis, G. (2011). *Multiversities, ideas, and democracy.* Toronto: University of Toronto Press.

Forbes-Mewett, H., & Nyland, C. (2008). Cultural diversity, relocation, and the security of international students at an internationalised university. *Journal of Studies in International Education, 12*(2), 181–203.

Fricker, M. (2007). *Epistemic injustice: Power and the ethics of knowing.* Oxford: Oxford University Press.

Gorski, P. C. (2008). Good intentions are not enough: A decolonizing intercultural education. *Intercultural Education, 19*(6), 515–525.

Gregory, M., & Gregory, M. V. (2013). *Teaching excellence in higher education.* London: Springer.

Gunn, V., & Fisk, A. (2013). *Considering teaching excellence in higher education: 2007–2013: A literature review since the CHERI Report 2007.* Accessed on 28 November 2018. Retrieved from http://eprints.gla.ac.uk/87987/1/87987.pdf.

Hazelkorn, E. (2015). *Rankings and the reshaping of higher education: The battle for world-class excellence.* London: Springer.

Kapoor, I. (2008). *The postcolonial politics of development.* London: Routledge.

Lynch, K., & Baker, J. (2005). Equality in education: An equality of condition perspective. *Theory and Research in Education, 3*(2), 131–164.

Marginson, S. (2012). Including the other: Regulation of the human rights of mobile students in a nation-bound world. *Higher Education, 63*(4), 497–512.

Marginson, S. (2015). *UK international education: Global position and national prospects.* Occasional paper delivered at the UK Council for International Students' Affairs (UKCISA) conference, University of Sussex. Accessed on 28 November 2018. Retrieved from https://www.ukcisa.org.uk/Research–Policy/Resource-bank/resources/86/UK-International-Education-global-position-and-national-prospects.

Mignolo, W. (2002). The geopolitics of knowledge and the colonial difference. *The South Atlantic Quarterly, 101*(1), 57–96.

Mignolo, W. D. (2005). *The idea of Latin America.* Oxford: Blackwell.

Mignolo, W. D. (2009). Epistemic disobedience, independent thought and decolonial freedom. *Theory, Culture & Society, 26*(7–8), 159–181.

Mignolo, W. (2011). *The darker side of western modernity: Global futures, decolonial options.* Durham: Duke University Press.

Perry, L. B., & Southwell, L. (2011). Developing intercultural understanding and skills: Models and approaches. *Intercultural Education, 22*(6), 453–466.

Pietsch, T. (2012). Imperial echoes. *Times Higher Education,* no. 2040, 41–45. Education Abstracts.

Quijano, A. (2000). Coloniality of power and Eurocentrism in Latin America. *International Sociology, 15*(2), 215–232.

Silva, D. F. (2015). Globality. *Critical Ethnic Studies, 1*(1), 33–38.

Skelton, A. (2005). *Understanding teaching excellence in higher education: Towards a critical approach.* London: Routledge.

Spivak, G. C. (1988). Can the subaltern speak? In R. C. Morris (Ed.), *Can the subaltern speak? Reflections on the history of an idea* (pp. 21–78). New York: Columbia University Press.

Stein, S., & de Andreotti, V. O. (2016). Decolonization and higher education. In M. Peters (Ed.), *Encyclopedia of Educational Philosophy and Theory* (pp. 1–6). Singapore: Springer.

Stein, S., Andreotti, V. D. O., & Suša, R. (2016). 'Beyond 2015', within the modern/colonial global imaginary? Global development and higher education. *Critical Studies in Education,* 1–21. https://doi.org/10.1080/1750848 7.2016.1247737.

Tannock, S. (2018). *Educational equality and international students.* London: Springer.

Taylor, C. (2004). *Modern social imaginaries.* Durham: Duke University Press.

The HE Commission. (2018). *Staying ahead: Are international students going down under?* Accessed on 28 November 2018. https://www.policyconnect.org.uk/hec/research/report-staying-ahead-are-international-students-going-down-under.

Wallerstein, I. (1997). Eurocentrism and its avatars: The dilemmas of social science. *Sociological Bulletin, 46*(1), 21–39.

Williams, P. (1984). Britain's full-cost policy for overseas students. *Comparative Education Review, 28*(2), 258–278.

4

Pedagogy as a Political Act Towards Epistemic Democracy—The Type of Understanding of Teaching Excellence the TEF Can Shape?

This chapter looks at the influence of marketisation of higher education on the TEF's cross-national equivalents (Assessment of Higher Education Learning Outcomes [AHELO], Comparing Achievements of Learning Outcomes in Higher Education in Europe [CALOHEE] and Collegiate Learning Assessment [CLA]) which, under this influence, and similarly to the TEF, do not aim to shape understandings of teaching excellence as including epistemic democracy. The chapter argues that they don't have to, as the current scope and nature of referents of internationalisation and teaching excellence do not require them to do so. The chapter also reviews ways in which commercialisation of higher education shapes understandings of teaching excellence as benchmarked-performativity. The key contribution of the chapter is an alternative proposal for metrics in these supra-national frameworks that is grounded in critical pedagogies and could instead shape understandings of teaching excellence as a political act towards social change that is more inclusive of international students.

Teaching has been widely identified in higher education literature as an area that has the greatest potential to transform relationships with international students and ensure their inclusion as equals (e.g. Lichan 2015; Tange and Kastberg 2013). Yet, metrics that are proposed to

© The Author(s) 2019
A. Hayes, *Inclusion, Epistemic Democracy and International Students,*
https://doi.org/10.1007/978-3-030-11401-5_4

'measure' the so called excellence in teaching, either nationally in the UK through the TEF, or internationally through projects such as AHELO, CALOHEE or the CLA, do not include any assessments of those aspects of teaching practice that critically engage with perspectives and identities of people beyond the nation state. In fact, as will be shown below, they do not include *any* assessments of teaching practice at all!

The very idea of attempting to measure excellence in teaching is also highly contentious, so are its various understandings and competing perspectives. But if excellence is understood from a critical pedagogy perspective (Freire 1970), as it is in this book, and is taken to mean excellence in teaching that is materialised as a political act to create social change towards inclusion of those who have been traditionally marginalised, then this book argues that it is possible to 'measure' excellence conceptualised in this way through the TEF. This would however require to position teaching excellence as *a process standard* in higher education. Chapter 5 discusses in detail how this can be done. This chapter prefaces some conceptual ideas pointing to the need for a TEF metric that will lead to a change in positioning of teaching excellence from an outcomes-based to a process-based phenomenon, in order to transcend and challenge the systemic hegemony that normalises commercialisation of higher education, and as a result, shapes understandings of teaching excellence as benchmarked-performativity.

The key point discussed in this chapter is that national governments and supra-national organisations can create an agreed frame for realisation of international students as epistemic equals and that, through this frame, they can also begin to shape understanding of excellent teaching as a process that triggers and sustains this realisation. This means challenging the hegemonic forces of current teaching assessment policies through designing a new ranking that is based on this frame. These governments and organisations must fight fire with fire and instead of continuing to challenge the symptoms of current policies regarding international students (which were discussed in Chapter 2), as well as their associated espoused values *after* they have crept into the public domain, they have a responsibility to create a ranking that will at least contraindicate some of these symptoms, and hopefully, in the long term prevent their re-production in the future. This chapter outlines the philosophical assumptions of such a ranking and conceptualises the meaning of teaching excellence it can evoke. This meaning is based around ideas of *teaching quality as consistency in delivering transformation.*

While on the one hand, universities, through encompassing internationalisation as one of its ideological principles, have more opportunities to pursue solidaristic and democratising approaches to international students, as they become increasingly connected with global people, they, on the other, do not do very well in fostering geographical, cultural and political mobility. It is argued in this book that this is because internationalisation, in the era of neoliberalism and marketisation of higher education, is not pursued under the influence of traditions whereby internationalisation is seen as an 'unalloyed' and 'pure' endeavour to produce liberal knowledge, preparing individuals to deal with the complexity of today's world, diversity and change (e.g. Britez and Peters 2010). It is rather seen as yet another one of the tendencies of 'multiversities', leading through misunderstandings in conceptualisation and articulation of university internationalisation.

The term 'multiversities' was developed by Clark Kerr (2001) to describe twenty-first century universities that evolve under conditions of economic growth and worldwide competition. As a result, they need to become more 'multi' in their nature and scope. 'Multiversities', as explained by Kerr (2001), are large conglomerates that have multiple purposes, of producing knowledge and offering services like never before. In that, they have become 'pluralistic in several senses: in having several purposes, not one; in having several centers of power, not one, in serving several clienteles, not one' (Kerr 2001, p. 103). Kerr (2001, p. 5) posits that 'multiversity is not a reasoned choice among elegant alternatives' but a consequence of an economic idea that is here to stay. This also affects internationalisation (Haapakoski and Pashby 2017). Perhaps that is why 'multiversities' have not become pluralistic in that one important sense that is the cornerstone of this book—that is, that of realisation of international students as epistemic equals. It is argued that this is because internationalisation that nowadays feeds organisational expansion of 'multiversities' does not require direct, functional and social changes in organisations, to generate resources for competition in the internationalisation 'category' of expansion (e.g. Farrell and Van Der Werf 2007; Haapakoski and Pashby 2017). Whilst for instance, university performance in the research category may involve new infrastructures, provision of information, institutional and international mergers, but also primarily the acceptance that 'others' are equal producers of knowledge, performance in the internationalisation category seems to be one that is a lot less demanding in this respect. Especially in the sense of social change accepting 'others' as equal, universities under their expansion to institutions that are more 'multi', are not required to be more inclusive of international students to compete for reputational privileges connected with internationalisation. As the current ranking stand, they simply need to recruit more international students.

Presently, internationalisation represents a category of performance that relies on structural measurements which do not require any social changes at universities. Structural indicators of levels of internationalisation developed by commercial organisations such as *Times Higher Education*, which include referents based on international-home students ratios and numbers of internationally co-authored publications, create reputational and expansion ends for universities that do not require them to commit to plurality in the sense of making international students politically, socially and intellectually equal. It has in fact been argued elsewhere that because presently, internationalisation is measured in terms of extensivity and intensivity of international students recruitment and internationally co-ordinated research projects and outputs, even universities with the most conservative cultures and deficit-orientated views towards international students can be assessed as highly internationalised (Hayes 2019).

The same applies to understandings of 'excellence in teaching' in multiversities. Teaching excellence is no longer viewed in Cardinal Newman's terms as a means to achieving liberal education, nor it is seen in Humboltian's understandings which emphasise excellent teaching as making new discoveries through research. Rather, teaching excellence in multiversities seems to be positioned as yet another means to winning national and international competition. As noted by Brockerhoff et al. (2014), whilst some time ago, assessing excellent teaching was mainly a matter for individual universities and was primarily an internal

4 Pedagogy as a Political Act Towards Epistemic Democracy ... 79

process of evaluation, it has nowadays become a mandatory process prescribed nationally by policymakers who view it as a means to winning institutional rivalry; both at the national level as well as internationally. In Germany, for example, these views have resulted in national initiatives such as *Wettbewerb Exzellente Lehre*, introduced in 2010 to establish a national competition framework for teaching excellence. Similar frameworks have also been established in Sweden and Finland (Brockerhoff et al. 2014), as well as outside of Europe, for example, in the USA, where institutions across all 50 states have been signing up to the CLA, a national evaluation exercise, drawn on to shape the TEF, that aims to 'compare the institutional effectiveness of curricula, programmes and teaching' (Mok 2017, p. 172). It is needless to say that the TEF has been influenced by similar competition undercurrents as 'the Government has introduced the TEF as a way of better informing students' choices about what and where to study, raising esteem for teaching, recognising and rewarding excellent teaching and better meeting the needs of employers, business, industry and the professions' (DfE 2018, p. 7). All to do with intentions for universities to become more multi.

The CLA has formed the basis of the OECD project AHELO, which in turn informed the design of the latest EU-wide initiative CALOHEE. The chapter is focused on these 3 assessment frameworks (CLA, AHELO and CALOHEE) because, like 'multiversities', they are networked projects and assessment conglomerates that represent a multi-polar nature of university landscape nowadays. Through their networked nature, as explained in Chapter 1, they are also likely to shape a dominant understanding of teaching excellence. In fact, as will be explained below, all of these 3 projects already suggest a degree of convergence and a common agreement about what teaching excellence is. This agreement however, does not include delivering just and free from coloniality education experiences and the components of CLA, AHELO and CALOHEE that are reviewed below do not suggest any potential for change in this area.

Teaching excellence can of course be defined in more than one way and, as shown in commentaries about the TEF so far, it can also be inadequately measured (e.g. Grove 2015; Derounian 2017). The purpose of this book is therefore to 'intervene', while there is still time, as the AHELO and CALOHEE projects have not yet been fully developed, and when the TEF is undergoing a consultation on its final form and shape (DfE 2018). Thus, the book intends to show that it is possible to design a supplementary TEF metric that could challenge the current understandings of teaching excellence and prompt the exercise, and its international equivalents, to also include epistemic democracy as one of its determinants. This will however require transcending the dominant policy hegemony that normalises understandings of quality of teaching without any attention to how the present misunderstandings and institutional mis-articulations of internationalisation prevent epistemic democracy. But, as already indicated above, this can only be done when governments create a metric that will prompt an alternative policy discourse about international students.

The book also intends to propose a model for assessment of excellence in teaching that will challenge the negative effects of exclusion of international students that are caused by universities' long connection to the nation state. As argued by Fallis (2011), on the one hand, the multiversity is the most global of institutions as its students and staff come from all over the world and its research findings and knowledge are applied internationally. However, as noted by Slaughter and Leslie (1997, p. 1), exposure to and influence of international people and networks is, on the other hand, 'destabilising patters of university professional work developed over the past hundred years', and universities feel threatened by internationalisation as it reduces their sovereignty and re-shape their identity. Universities have always had a profoundly national character and have been symbolically linked to their countries' histories, politics and society (for latest review, see Buckner 2017). This connection means that current speed of internationalisation under strategies to become more 'multi' must create tensions within multiversities, arising from having to find the balance between national values and having to become more cosmopolitan. It has been argued by Marginson (2013, p. 13) that such tensions result in the inability of governments to manage cultural plurality, which is why the public are more 'comfortable with the notions of global persons as economic subjects than as plural cultural subjects'. These notions however result in lower status of foreign students in the classroom and the lack of state support to 'upgrade' them to 'equals'. Writing in the context of how multiversities develop into world class universities (WCU) through internationalisation and influences of globalisation, Marginson (2018) noted that:

> Beyond the national border, there is no standard framework for addressing questions of equity in WCUs. There is no global polity, nor a single global educational population, for fixing benchmarks of representative social composition or affirmative action strategy. Operating in the global space, WCUs, and individual persons may practise fairness and justice but only on the basis of eclectic, self-proclaimed principles that create no obligations for others. There is no means to devise an agreed rule. The result is that when cross-border activity triggers equity issues within countries [*and university classrooms – my emphasis*], or issues of fairness arise in relations between countries [*or between students and teachers in university classrooms – my emphasis*] (…)these are not effectively addressed. (Marginson 2018, p. 70)

This book argues that the TEF, AHELO, CALOHEE and even the CLA could constitute such agreed rules which would create obligations *for all* within universities to realise international students as equals and to insist on the establishment and maintenance of intellectually just conditions for their participation in higher education. Presently however, such obligations do not constitute plans for the final shape of AHELO and CALOHEE, nor are they discussed as possible changes to the CLA (I focus on the TEF in detail in Chapter 5). CLA for instance, which is an already established assessment framework in the US, focuses exclusively on the evaluation of analytical reasoning, critical thinking, problem solving and written communication skills. The nature and scope of the tasks that are used in the CLA to assess these skills are analysed in Chapter 6 (to contrast them with the proposed model for the TEF) but here it is worth highlighting the specific ways in which CLA functions as a teaching assessment tool that frames benchmarked-based understanding of teaching excellence, as it only measures whether students pass a set of minimum standards or not. Quality of teaching under CLA is therefore contingent on students' performance against benchmarks that subsequently define what high standard of teaching is. But, as explained in more detail in the section below, there is no evaluation of value added, the nature of pedagogy, nor the *relationality* between them. The outcomes that are measured by the CLA are not in any way related to ways in which universities create conditions for intellectually just, democratic and equitable education for all students. And because such outcomes are not part of the CLA, nobody holds universities accountable for how well they fulfil these conditions.

The influence of commercialisation of multiversities on the CLA is clear in that the exercise seems to be based on auditing university outputs (understood as good performance of their students), which introduces a system of organisational regulation through accountability and performance, and for purposes of competition.

> The CLA focuses on the institution (rather than the student) as the unit of analysis. (…) The results are intended to send a signal to administrators, faculty and the students about some of the competencies that need to be developed, the level of performance attained by the students at their institution and most importantly, whether that level is better, worse or about the same as what would be expected given the ability level of its incoming students. (…) Because the CLA scores are standardised across administrations, they can be used (along with other indicators) to examine the overall effects on student performance of the reforms and policies an institution implements. In short, the CLA's main goal is to provide information that will help colleges and universities determine how much their students are improving and whether that improvement is in line with the gains of comparable students at other institutions. (Klein et al. 2007, p. 418)

The above description of the CLA makes it clear what matters in higher education and that the worth of a university is determined by its graduates' performance meeting or exceeding certain benchmarks. Only then the university is seen as 'high quality', with these benchmarks having little (or nothing) to do with the teaching process. This worth reflects how universities change under the influence of neo-liberalism, from being a

4 Pedagogy as a Political Act Towards Epistemic Democracy ...

centre of critical citizenship learning to becoming a 'business organisation with productivity targets' (Doring 2002, p.140).

AHELO, while temporarily put on hold, seems to be driven by similar targets. The project's website states that 'more than a ranking, the AHELO assessment aims to be direct evaluation of student performance at the global level and valid across diverse cultures, languages and different types of institutions'. Such goals do not suggest evaluations of institutions and teaching based on democratic merits, but rather focus on targets that are operational. Indeed, this seems to be clearly manifested in AHELO's assessment tasks that test generic skills common to all students (such as critical thinking, analytical reasoning, problem-solving, and written communication) and discipline-specific skills in economics and engineering, with student performance on both sets of skills being interpreted in relation to their backgrounds and learning environments. There is nothing wrong with such skills and their development should by all means be supported by universities, but the fact that only these types of skills are measured in AHELO signifies what matters in university teaching. AHELO therefore directs attention to 'measured' outputs, rather than the nature and scope of the education process or pedagogy. The focus is clearly on organisational performativity that becomes coded by AHELO outcomes and marketed as an indication of teaching quality. The following caution, for instance, has been issued in relation to such effects of AHELO.

> It is important that large-scale international assessments such as AHELO do not start to colonialise and converge understandings of what is considered a desirable end result, promote conceptions of 'good' teaching and learning in higher education and hence become intentionally a powerful political tool to steer and justify national educational reforms (Ursin 2015, p. i)

Ursin (2015) further argues that the rationale for AHELO lies in the global competition trends, which aim to tease out differences in diversification of institutional profiles and student body, differing levels of internationalisation, as well as the growing emphasis on market forces in higher education. These factors, according to Ursin (2015) are likely to profoundly change what matters about teaching in higher education. If used for marketing purposes, AHELO results will inevitably become a ranking which will devalue moral values of teaching in higher education, especially those that could emphasise that international people are not strangers but rather valued and intellectually equal members of the classroom community. Universities therefore run the risk of being subordinated to marketised principles of performativity that will 're-orient pedagogical and scholarly activities towards those which are likely to have a positive impact on measurable performance outcomes and are a deflection of attention away from aspects of social, emotional and moral development that have no immediate measurable performance value' (Ball 2012, p. 20).

The added complication is that well-meaning individuals whose teaching is based around emotional, social and moral development at universities will not be able to single-handedly change the marketised policy hegemony that tells them to do otherwise. That is why the arguments in this book are based on the view that the best way forward is to create a ranking that will encompass, and officially 'measure', all those social, emotional and moral development pedagogies that could lead to greater inclusion of international students and prompt liberation of home students from the oppression of public policy discourses that prevent them from developing reciprocal relationships with their international peers. At least then, those who are committed to practising education that prevents coloniality will have the backing from the political power. And if such backing is enacted through official rankings frameworks, it will additionally create obligations for others to do so as well.

Those who oppose rankings are likely to oppose the ideas in this book too. The truth however is that we have no choice but to comply with the rankings as they continue to drive profound transformations of our higher education systems and institutions (Hazelkorn 2015). They also bring financial, reputational and social rewards to universities and will therefore not go away. So, why not create rankings that will 'measure' how universities promote epistemic democracy for international students, but also through that, how they simultaneously contribute to epistemic development of home students? At least then, we will have an

4 Pedagogy as a Political Act Towards Epistemic Democracy … 85

agreed frame that will shape espoused values about teaching in higher education, emphasising that 'excellence' also means creating conditions for intellectual equity for all members of the classroom community. Such a frame will also help to materialise the long-standing commitment of universities to civic development and improving democratic lives of their participants. This commitment has always been included in painting the university landscape but has rarely materialised. We therefore need to make room for it, not only in our hearts and minds, but also in university rankings.

The third project that this book discusses, CALOHEE, offers some hope that teaching which supports political, social and cultural equity is at least being discussed as part of this new EU ranking.

There are four assessment strands underlying CALOHEE and they give some indication of EU plans to assess civic responsibilities of universities to create just and equitable participation in higher education for all. These four strands include: (1) Knowledge (Theory and Methodology), (2) Applying Knowledge and Skills, (3) Preparing for Employability and (4) *Civic, Social and Cultural Engagement*. It is under this fourth strand that the creators of CALOHEE attempt to develop assessments that will 'measure' student competencies in terms of interculturalism, conflict management, processes of communication, governance and decision making, as well as ethics, norms, values and professional standards (CALOHEE Working Paper 2017, p. 7). These assessments, whilst being, at least indirectly linked to principles of epistemic democracy, do not however include, as will be shown below, any estimations of the contribution of the teaching process to the competencies listed.

The CALOHEE working paper for Civic, Social and Cultural Engagement positions that barriers affecting multicultural integration include the lack of tolerance of other cultures and religions, as well as the lack of confidence in many cultural groups as 'valid'. The paper uses these barriers to justify the need for developing assessments focusing on 'civic and social competencies', including 'cultural awareness and expression' and 'intercultural competence that cover all forms of behaviour that equip individuals to participate in an effective and constructive way in social and working life, and particularly in increasingly diverse societies' (CLOHEE Working Paper 2017, p. 3). Unlike other assessments discussed so far, CALOHEE is the only project that seems to acknowledge that under the influence of 'fear' from other, social and cultural engagement has suffered and that it should be a concern for higher education institutions to address. 'Although, it has been promoted that higher education has an obvious role in preparing students for active citizenship, in practice it is not part of (most) existing curricula, at least not made explicit in the outcomes of the formal learning programmes' (CALOHEE Working Paper 2017, p. 3). That is why the fourth strand of CALOHEE of Civic, Social and Cultural Engagement proposes to assess the following competencies (see Table 4.1), which require 'an attitude of collaboration, assertiveness and integrity. Individuals should have an interest in socio-economic developments and intercultural communication and should value diversity and respect others, and be prepared both to overcome prejudices and to compromise' (ibid., p. 3). Still, there is no proposition here to assess the teaching process that contributes to these competencies.

The competencies listed in Table 4.1 are in many ways akin to the basis for the TEF metric that this book proposes, but with the main difference being that the latter actually proposes to assess the contribution of the teaching process to the development of students' civic competencies. CALOHEE seems to be assessing just the outcomes alone, i.e. whether they have been achieved by the students or not, which prompts the same concerns as those raised in relation to AHELO or CLA about quality of teaching being understood as meeting certain 'standards' and 'thresholds'. The model for the TEF metrics proposed in this book is however different in that it changes understandings of teaching quality as meeting 'fixed' standards to one that emphasises quality *as consistency in delivering transformation* (Harvey 2006).

Harvey's (2006) theorisations about what quality as consistency means are helpful in explaining the type of 'measurement' captured by the proposed metric in this book. First of all, *teaching quality as consistency in delivering transformation* requires a shift from measuring outcomes that already exist or can be achieved independently of the teaching process (I discuss this in more details in Chapter 6) to measuring *process* standards (Harvey 2006). Unlike the outcomes that are

Table 4.1 CALOHEE framework for Civic, Social and Cultural Engagement (Adapted from CALOHEE Working Paper 2017, p. 7—https://www.calohee.eu/wp-content/uploads/2016/06/Working-Paper-for-Civic-Social-and-Cultural-Engagement.pdf)

Knowledge	Skills	Wider competences
Demonstrate critical understanding of differences in and between societies and cultures (frames)	Identify, describe and analyse issues in and between societies and cultures	Demonstrate engagement by developing scenarios and alternatives for identifying best practices and interventions in the case of tensions and conflicts
Demonstrate critical understanding of the processes of information and communication	Review and judge (mis)use of sources, data, evidence, qualities, intentions and transparency and expert opinions	Active contribution to societal debates using reliable data and information sources and informed judgements
Demonstrate critical understanding of the processes of governance and decision making	Apply and support agreed governing principles, norms and values regarding fairness, transparency, accountability, democracy and relevance in policy making processes	Active contribution to and with local and (inter)national communities, community groups, (political) organisations and pressure groups respecting agreed principles, norms and values
Demonstrate critical understanding of general ethical principles, norms and values and professional standards	Understand and apply the processes of decision making and the consequences of actions taking into account principles, norms, values and standards both from a personal and a professional standpoint	Active contribution to upholding, promoting and defending general ethical principles, norms, values and professional standards in governance, communication and cultural interaction

listed, for instance, in the Table 4.1, which can arguably be achieved without any input from the teaching process, process standards which are proposed to be measured by changes to the TEF discussed in this book, on the other hand, are explicitly linked to teaching processes in that they emphasise the role of pedagogies in creating a specific educational situation. In the context of this book, the standards of interest are *equal, just and unprejudiced inclusion* in the classroom community. Achieving these standards means consistently maintaining them, through adequate pedagogies, where they already exist or leading to transformation in the classroom culture where they are absent; and then maintaining them afterwards. These standards are not measured by any external indicators, nor there is a cut off point for them. The transformation that is either started or maintained is therefore not assessed against any benchmarks but what rather matters is that it is consistently delivered. In that sense, these standards are not an end in itself, but rather a means towards consistently delivering democratic conditions for international students participation. Chapters 5 and 6 explain how the proposed model for the TEF metric on internationalisation supports such means. Generally speaking, the model is based on the philosophy of prevention, rather than inspection, to make sure that the quality of realising international students as intellectual equals is maintained and, where it has not yet been identified, encouraged. The aim of the proposed TEF metric, functioning in national rankings as a referent of teaching that is applied year on year, is therefore to prevent realisation of students as epistemic equals from fading away or dying down as opposed to developing benchmarks that would identify whether it is practised or not.

Teaching quality as consistency in delivering transformation therefore 'turns quality into a relative concept. There are no absolutes against which the output can be assessed, nor are there any universal benchmarks' (Harvey 2006, p. 7). The sample metric in Chapter 7 is based on this turn, in that it shows whether the teaching process on student courses is characterised by pedagogies that encourage inclusion and what role teaching on a particular course plays in students' sense of belonging as 'equal' members of the classroom community. There is however no 'target' standard for levels of this inclusion, the metric rather identifies the consistency and continuation of its practice. The aim here is to show that it is practised and to ensure, through continuous assessments in subsequent TEF assessments, that it has been practised throughout the years. Setting a 'target' standard or a 'benchmark' (based on classroom specifications) for measuring inclusion would be daft and technically invalid as it would be difficult to talk about 'levels' of inclusion in objective terms and also because classrooms each year are likely to have different 'specifications' (for example, in terms of home-international students' ratios or the content taught). Rather the point is to show that each classroom performs *to its own* specifications, evaluating epistemic democracy as a relative concept. When used in individual national contexts, for instance, the metric would still compare universities' commitment to epistemic democracy but not according to their performance on some arbitrary benchmarks, but rather based on what they are doing, and how, to achieve greater epistemic democracy. The proposed metric could therefore be developed based on any national data that capture, at least to some extent, the relationship between teaching and inclusivity (the example in Chapter 7 uses UKES), also including more diverse populations that may be experiencing issues arising from their undemocratic treatment. These populations could include indigenous communities or non-traditional students. All countries would however be assessing the same core idea—that is, whether socially just, unprejudiced and free from coloniality education is practised.

The core idea that the proposed TEF metric assesses is drawn from the tradition of critical pedagogy. It builds on the work of Paulo Freire (1970) who argues that education should be a means to emancipation of those who have traditionally been marginalised and oppressed (here international students). For Freire, such emancipation can happen via praxis—i.e. reflection and action upon the world in order to transform it (Freire 1970). This transformation is further achieved through conscientização (conscientization)—that is raising critical consciousness of people through dialogue and group discussions that problematise the lives of the oppressed and represent these lives to them and their oppressors (here home students) for critical analysis (ibid.). Conscientization therefore can be seen to represent 'transformative work in politics and

90   A. Hayes

pedagogy [which] involves a challenge to the modes of cognition, affective structures and constitutive relationships that delimit the ways of being of students and teachers (De Lissovoy 2018, p. 187).

Since Freire, conscientization, praxis and critical pedagogy have been widely used in inclusive education literature to advocate for pedagogy that enables students, especially those from diverse backgrounds and those 'oppressed' in any ways, to use their experiences, values, and identities to provide an important means for collective empowerment and social change in education (e.g. Khan and Gabriel 2018; Guilherme 2017; Roets et al. 2012). Freire (1970) has argued that critical pedagogy can achieve social change of greater inclusivity for those who have been oppressed in education because it lays bare the power relations and hegemony as it 'deal[s] with the problem of the oppressed consciousness and the oppressor consciousness, the problem of men and women who oppress and men and women who suffer oppression. It must take into account their behavior; their view of the world, and their ethics' (Freire 1970, p. 55). All of this happens through praxis which produces counter-hegemony based on the view that:

> (…) the oppressed are not 'marginals', are not people living 'outside' society. They have always been 'inside' — inside the structure which made them 'beings for others'. The solution is not to 'integrate' them into the structure of oppression, but to transform that structure so that they can become 'beings for themselves'. (Freire 1970, p. 74)
>
> [But] the central problem is this: How can the oppressed, as divided, unauthentic beings, participate in developing the pedagogy of their liberation? Only as they discover themselves to be 'hosts' of the oppressor can they contribute to the midwifery of their liberating pedagogy. As long as they live in the duality in which *to be* is *to be like*, and *to be like* is *to be like the oppressor*, this contribution is impossible. (Freire 1970, p. 48)

The above ways in which Freire (1970) summarises the philosophical basis of critical pedagogy sit comfortably with the conceptual basis underpinning the model for the TEF metric proposed in this book. In the current climate of rankings, and the lack of proposals for national and cross-national assessment criteria that include evaluations of critical

4 Pedagogy as a Political Act Towards Epistemic Democracy ... 91

pedagogy, the proposed metric has never been more important. The intention of the proposed metric is to evaluate whether teachers teach their students to evaluate beliefs, values and ethics within their own education tradition, but also those drawn from another viewpoint. It intends to evaluate, to use Freire's (1970) words, how teachers teach their students to 'discover themselves' through engaging with intellects of others who are different. Such intentions justify the choice of the UKES items that are selected for the metric. Those items are focused on skills in engaging with students from other backgrounds but also on their ability to develop and express their own views and ethics (these items are deconstructed in more detail in Chapter 6).

More contemporary writers such as Tran and Vu (2017), for instance, call the type of simultaneous expression of own views and positions discussed by Freire which engage with positions of others, 'social responsibility'. Tran and Vu (2017) argue that being in educational mobility provides international students with unique transnational social fields to develop responsibility towards the home and host countries. This, aside responsibilities of being ambassadors to their home countries, also means that when international students are self-positioned as members of the host community, they take on responsibilities of contributing to and representing this community. If, on the other hand, they position themselves, or are positioned as 'outsiders', they are more likely to feel they need to be assimilated (ibid.). Such conclusions sit comfortably with Freire's (1970) argument that through assimilation, the oppressed 'confuse freedom with the maintenance of the *status quo*' (p. 10) and through 'remaining passive in the face of the oppressors' violence', (...) they accept the state of oppression that gratifies the oppressor (p. 11). It happens because taking refuge (through assimilation) is an attempt to achieve security, which is preferred by the oppressed to the risks of liberty (Freire 1970). Such 'thinking' of the oppressed was revealed in Chapter 1, where the excerpts from the students' interviews showed that taking refuge via routes that offered emotional wellbeing was a preferred option, as opposed to seeking liberty via exercising anti-discrimination laws.

But this means that universities and the state have an extra important role in re-shaping international students' responsibilities and the ways in

92   A. Hayes

which they enact them. As argued by Tran and Vu (2017), the responsibility to facilitate this lies within institutions which, influenced by neoliberal commercialisation, have drifted away from building student capacities for ending their oppression through responsible engagement with host communities:

> The locus of institutional responsibility should therefore extend beyond simply providing the educational services to actually enabling international students to develop full capacity to enact responsibility in educationally, culturally and morally productive ways. In order to achieve this, it is important for host institutions to ensure the productive conditions and external opportunities for international students to exercise responsibility as intercultural members and learners. It is also imperative for host institutions not to ignore the ways in which student mobility intersects with personal agency and personal capacity as well as multiple and transnational logics of legal, social, cultural and academic practices in viewing international student responsibility. (Tran and Vu 2017, p. 573)

Hence, the insistence in this book that the solution to the oppressor-oppressed situation does not lie in 'a mere reversal of position, in moving from one pole to another. Nor does it lie in the replacement of the former oppressors with new ones who continue to subjugate the oppressed, all in the name of their liberation' (Freire 1970, p. 31). That is why the book cautions about pedagogies of reparation—in the sense of trying to induce the reversal of the roles of the oppressed and the oppressors through overemphasising identities of international students because universities, for instance, feel guilty about the oppression they have caused them. Rather, the book insists that universities begin to encourage changes in international students' positioning (self or institutional) towards the oppressor through providing structures that will produce a counter narrative to old logics of legal, cultural and policy frames that encourage international students to assimilate. These changes can be encouraged by the proposed metric as it will introduce a modus operandi whereby international students will be taught to think about themselves as 'equals'. Such modus operandi will also lead to teachers' 'self-actualization' (Hooks 2014) as it will reveal how much the teachers care for the souls of the students and how through that, they become aware of who they are as teachers (hooks 2014)—that is, whether they teach in a non-discriminatory and empowering way. Such teaching is in line with Freire's (1970) idea of praxis—i.e. reflection on self and others to change the world. In Madge et al.'s words (2009), this would mean beginning to think responsibly about international students, in Tran and Vu's (2017) view, this would be enacted by giving them structures that enable their 'social responsibility'. Thus, the key concept underlying the proposed metric is *transformation*. It is analysed below in relation to understandings of teaching excellence it can evoke.

Notions of 'Teaching Excellence' Evoked by the Proposed TEF Metrics

The focus on transformation in the proposed TEF metric is purposeful; firstly, to create opportunities to disembed assessments of teaching from neo-liberalism that drives the standard- or benchmark-based understandings of teaching quality and secondly, to create value, and a dedicated 'space' in national exercises related to measuring teaching quality for assessments of teaching based on critical pedagogy (in the sense explained in the previous section). The focus on transformation in the proposed changes to the TEF therefore distinguishes these changes from the existing TEF referents primarily in that it evokes understandings of teaching excellence as the degree to which universities 'develop people'. Currently, the TEF implies understanding of excellence as being performance based and its current metrics do not even focus on the performance of the teachers, but rather on students' performance on 'benchmarks' which is then adjusted for their individual characteristics, such as their socio-economic backgrounds and ethnicity. These standards and their associated understandings of 'excellence' have nothing to do with how universities and tutors transform people. They are rather about excelling in benchmark-based outputs.

It is also difficult to conceive how the process by which students learn (and transform!) is considered in the current TEF metrics, as the analysis of the NSS ratings for instance (which is one of the metrics in the current TEF), contains no information about the contribution of the teaching process to student satisfaction levels with aspects of their courses. It has been argued by the creators of the TEF that the 'split metrics' provide indications of the 'value added', as through the analysis of performance of universities in terms of, for instance, how well widening participation (WP) students do, the TEF could be a new assessment of:

> (…) the journey travelled. If the university is taking students predominantly from disadvantaged backgrounds with lower A levels and is then getting them into graduate jobs and giving them real cognitive gain, that achievement is not caught by current league tables. (David Willetts, cited in Morgan 2015)

Such analyses, however, limit understandings of teaching quality to attaining criteria that have been designed for universities to ensure minimum standards, considering the characteristics of the intake of their students. Still not much is captured here in terms of value added.

This book therefore proposes 'measurements' of excellence that are not institutionally-defined and based on minimal quality standards, but ones that evaluate transformations—in the sense of how students and teachers are engaged and work together towards an understanding that epistemic democracy in the classroom leads to critically-informed value added to students' educational experiences and life-long skills. The proposed TEF metric in Part III of the book offer a contrast to the exercise's current measurements of institutional performance and proposes assessments of educational gains of students. These gains are understood as the validity of student judgement on curriculum content matters but also on whether this validity is carried out on reciprocal basis, involving mutually respectful positioning of home and international students as intellectual 'equals'.

Currently, through the threshold-based 'excellence' standards, the TEF assumes that teaching at universities can be improved if thresholds are raised. This is false and inadequate as, needless to say, attainment of individual students often depends on factors beyond teaching and

4 Pedagogy as a Political Act Towards Epistemic Democracy … 95

learning. The threshold-based approach also assumes that there is no other value of attending university but high grades, which consequently is commonly assumed to lead to better employment. But what about assessing *what else* is learnt and taught at university, in terms of social and personal development of individuals, especially when higher education institutions are expanded and diversified by the characteristics of their students? What social transformations are taking place in students and tutors and are they able to acknowledge the value of relationalities between themselves and global people that are now part of their education communities? Approaches to assessing 'excellence' based on these questions would have to involve assessments of transformations of staff and students that are qualitative and process-like in nature—that is, ones that accept international people as equally qualified 'knowers'.

In their seminal paper about quality of teaching in higher education as transformation, Harvey and Green (1993) asserted that transformation in teaching refers to the enhancement and empowerment of students or the development of new knowledge. They further argued that such transformations occur through the learning process and can also apply to changes within institutions so that universities can provide better support for any transformative learning experiences. Eckel et al. (1998, p. 3) agreed and asserted that 'transformation (1) alters the culture of an institution by changing select underlying assumptions and institutional behaviours, processes and products; (2) is deep and pervasive, affecting the whole institution; (3) is intentional and (4) occurs over time. Below, I use Eckel and colleagues' (1998) definition and conceptualisations of transformations as an analytical frame to explain why and how the proposed TEF metrics could set new process-based understandings of teaching excellence in higher education.

Transformation is grounded in shifts in an institutional culture (understood as a common set of beliefs which shape an agreed interpretation and understanding of activities and leadership decisions). Such shared interpretations and understandings are mostly evoked through policies such as the TEF which, as explained in Chapter 1, function as a discursive power that provide an official vehicle for realising stakeholder intentions and reflect their planned rationality. Through such functions, policies therefore shape understandings of what activities are acceptable

96   A. Hayes

and why. Eckel et al. (1998, p. 3) call these effects 'institution-wide patterns of perceiving, thinking, and feeling; shared understandings; collective assumptions; and common interpretive frameworks [which] are the ingredients of institutional culture'. Policies therefore function as organizational 'artifacts'—that is the 'the products, activities, and processes that form the landscape of the institution's culture' (Eckel et al. 1998, p. 3). Examples of these artifacts can include management patterns, governance decisions or reward structures. The TEF, therefore, being a reform that carries specific rewards in terms of reputations, and potential improvements, especially in international students' recruitment (see Chapter 5), can also be seen as one of those 'artifacts'. As such, the whole TEF exercise is a project that 'makes up' institutions and their espoused values. These 'espoused values', as Eckel et al. (1998, p. 3) argue 'are what we say—the articulated beliefs about what is "good," what "works," and what is "right."' The TEF, therefore, is an exercise that expects us to 'live' within the environment of teaching excellence 'made up' by its metrics and to abide by its rules.

The problem arises when the 'artifact' that drives the articulation of certain espoused values is linked to marketised and politised university competition games (as this book argues is the case with the TEF). This means that university tutors might say they promote something, but in fact might want to say or do something else. Of course, it might as well be the case that people agree with some of the 'espoused values', and that is fine, if they are internally convinced that market expansion, competition and their associated understandings of teaching quality are good and work for universities, especially when it comes to ignoring epistemic inclusion of international students. But in the context of the main argument in this chapter—that market pressures driving developments in the TEF prevent the exercise from 'measuring' the transformational quality of teaching—those of us who believe that teaching excellence should involve elements of transformation of students, and 'self' (as a university tutor), are faced with a difficulty in effecting these values because the present TEF 'artifacts' that create rules for thinking about teaching excellence seem to contradict them.

Such contradictory effects of policies and individual values have been highlighted by Gorski (2008) as the main barrier to intercultural education. Gorski (2008) argues that despite unquestionably good intentions on the part of most people who truly believe in intercultural education (in the democratic sense developed in this book), most intercultural education practice supports, rather than challenges, the dominant policy hegemony and the social hierarchies and inequalities established by neoliberalism surrounding internationalisation. The education systems, through its policies and the influence of those who govern them, 'have become tools for socialising a compliant and complicit populace into a market hegemony that normalises consumer culture, glorifies corporate imperialism and conflates capitalism with democracy' (Gorski 2008, p. 518). That is why, 'a philosophy of intercultural education that insists, first and foremost, on the establishment and maintenance of an equitable and just world [which is discussed in the book in the context of transformations] (...) cannot be achieved through intercultural programs or slight curricular shifts' (Gorski 2008, p. 524). Most of what people refer to as intercultural or multicultural education involves nothing more than such curricular shifts or 'intercultural communication' programmes (e.g. World Festivals or Chinese Movie Nights). But in their minds (and often against their will), universities are still not prepared to accept international students as equals because of the hegemonic artifacts and its associated 'espoused values' that socialise them into such superficial and tokenistic approaches to intercultural education. This is not their fault, but in the present climate, everything else is faced with resistance.

There is therefore no point putting our energies into challenging the symptoms of these artifacts and the espoused values they produce. Instead these energies should be relocated to challenging the artifacts themselves. How can this be done? *Through changes in what the artifacts prescribe for people to do.* This will trigger shifts in institutional consciousness that will start to acknowledge the need for epistemic democracy. And if this need is acknowledged, it will inform shifts in practice as a first step to authentic inclusion of international students. The creators of the TEF therefore need to raise questions about power and privilege and who, through the present state of the exercise's metrics, they marginalise or empower. The attention to deficits of international students in policy discourse needs to be turned away, to establish higher levels of congruence between the 'artifact', the 'espoused values' and authentically democratic integration of international students. Challenging the dominant hegemony is difficult, but it can be done through proposals and the model for the TEF metric discussed in Part III of this book.

The model in Part III is likely to create change that is pervasive through telling 'organisations what to do, how to behave, and what to produce', as this will start a change that is 'far-reaching within the institution' (Eckel et al. 1998, p. 4). It is argued throughout this book that if the TEF includes the metric that is proposed, it is likely to start 'modifications' in areas of articulating internationalisation and, subsequently, of teaching excellence because as such, it will consider internationalisation, understood as a process towards achieving epistemic democracy, as one of its determinants. The proposed model for the new TEF metric offers opportunities to re-articulate the structural focus in referents of internationalisation, shaped by commercial rankings, by focusing university's attention on commitment to plurality and creating an agreed frame for acceptance of 'others' as epistemic equals. Through that, the TEF, being a discursive power and a major 'artifact', can help socialise universities into thinking about international students in terms that emphasise their realisation as fellow participants in higher education, not as 'marginals'. The new TEF metrics are therefore based around such questions as 'How can universities show the extent to which epistemic engagement with international students is associated with the characteristics of the teaching process?' and, as alluded to in Chapter 1, 'How can they show the benefits of this engagement for home students as well?' If the answers to such questions are the basis of the TEF assessment, they will need to encompass an intention that will lead to specific outcomes in terms of transformations from tokenistic approaches to intercultural education and commercial focus on internationalisation to education that is *just, inclusive and free from coloniality*. Such outcomes are theorised by Eckel et al. (1998) under the intentionality aspect of transformation, meaning that, the TEF metrics that insist on the establishment and maintenance of equitable and just conditions for international students inclusion in the classroom will obligate universities to act and provide guidance in terms of the direction in which to act.

4 Pedagogy as a Political Act Towards Epistemic Democracy ... 99

So the key word accompanying the focus on transformation in the proposed metric is 'engagement'. 'Engagement' has been chosen because, as explained by Madge et al. (2009), what matters in teaching excellence understood as transformation is based on 'engaged pedagogy'. Madge et al.'s (2009) theorisations about 'engaged pedagogy' also effectively capture key ideas about critical pedagogy developed in the previous section and seems to be more of a modern version of Freire's (1970) ideas about creating social change. Madge et al.'s (2009) theorisations about 'engaged pedagogy' evolve around five key notions. The first one contests the centre from which care and responsibility towards international students can be talked about and experienced. This means 'consideration of how the categories of teacher and student are being affirmed, but also how they can be challenged' (Madge et al. 2009, p. 43). This implies transformation through engagement with new people. The second notion rests on the idea of a genuine dialogue, 'one that must contest the hegemonic discourse of Western 'best-practice' and at minimum to care and imagine everyday academic practices from a multitude of different perspectives and centres' (Madge et al. 2009, p. 43). This also implies transformation through engagement with new perspectives. The third notion mandates academics to take this new practice beyond the walls of their classrooms. The fourth one posits that this practice cannot be 'conceived a priori as it is necessarily deeply contextual and place specific' (Madge et al. 2009, p. 43). The book has already alluded to the ways in which the proposed metric could reduce the influence of the historical and political 'priori' on engagement with international students, through detaching the proposed metric from the dominant policy representations of international students and focusing instead on the assessment of process standards—that is, transformations that are taking place according to each classroom's own specifications. Finally, the fifth notion in Madge et al.'s (2009) framework cautions against the quandaries that may prevent engaged pedagogy, which, as argued by the authors, can be stopped if academics recognise their own weaknesses and limitations. Thus, this last principle also implies transformation—one that happens within self but also in others, so that institutional factors, histories of countries that may impose specific power relations and personal ethics do not affect interdependence and mutuality (i.e. intellectual engagement) which should underlie tutor relationships with international students.

The US, for instance, have adopted student engagement as one of the national indicators of *teaching quality as transformation*, by creating the National Survey of Student Engagement (NSSE). The NSSE has been used as a model in the UK, to create UKES, which in turn has been used to conceptualise the core design of the proposed metric in this book. Through the focus on students engagement, it has been possible in the book to discuss the philosophical basis of the proposed TEF metric that could help assess whether the teaching process on students' courses actively encourages international and home students to be engaged in one another's intellectual traditions, in ways that enable both to emphasise their own values and ethics about the topic. This is discussed in more detail in the next chapter.

References

Ball, S. J. (2012). Performativity, commodification and commitment: An I-spy guide to the neoliberal university. *British Journal of Educational Studies, 60*(1), 17–28.

Britez, R., & Peters, M. A. (2010). Internationalization and the cosmopolitical university. *Policy Futures in Education, 8*(2), 201–216.

Brockerhoff, L., Stensaker, B., & Huisman, J. (2014). Prescriptions and perceptions of teaching excellence: A study of the national 'Wettbewerb Exzellente Lehre' initiative in Germany. *Quality in Higher Education, 20*(3), 235–254.

Buckner, E. S. (2017). The changing discourse on higher education and the nation-state, 1960–2010. *Higher Education, 74*(3), 473–489.

CALOHEE Working Paper. (2017). *CALOHEE working paper for civic, social and cultural engagement.* Accessed 12 July 2018. Retrieved from https://www.calohee.eu/wp-content/uploads/2016/06/Working-Paper-for-Civic-Social-and-Cultural-Engagement.pdf.

De Lissovoy, N. (2018). Pedagogy of the anxious: Rethinking critical pedagogy in the context of neoliberal autonomy and responsibilization. *Journal of Education Policy, 33*(2), 187–205.

DfE (Department for Education). (2018). *Teaching Excellence and Student Outcomes Framework: Subject-level Consultation document.* Accessed on 02 Mar 2019. Available from https://consult.education.gov.uk/higher-education-reform/teaching-excellence-and-student-outcomes-framework/supporting_documents/Teaching%20Excellence%20and%20Student%20Outcomes%20Framework%20subjectlevel.pdf.

Derounian, J. 2017. TEF-tiresomely extraneous & flawed? *Compass: Journal of Learning and Teaching, 10*(2), 21–25.

Doring, A. (2002). Challenges to the academic role of change agent. *Journal of Further and Higher Education, 26*(2), 139–148.

Eckel, P., Hill, B., & Green, M. F. (1998). *En route to transformation.* Washington, DC: American Council on Education.

Fallis, G. (2011). *Multiversities, ideas, and democracy.* Toronto: University of Toronto Press.

Farrell, E., & Van Der Werf, M. (2007, May 25). Playing the rankings game. *Chronicle of Higher Education.* http://inthenews.unt.edu/sites/default/files/PDF/2007/5/25/05_25_2007_CHE_RankingsReport.pdf.

Freire, P. (1970). *Pedagogy of the oppressed* (M. B. Ramos, Trans.). New York: Continuum (published as Penguin Classics 2017).

Gorski, P. C. (2008). Good intentions are not enough: A decolonizing intercultural education. *Intercultural education, 19*(6), 515–525.

Grove, J. (2015). NSS results unrelated to teaching quality, study claims. *Times Higher Education.* Accessed on 12 July 2018. Retrieved from https://www.timeshighereducation.com/news/nss-results-unrelated-teaching-quality-study-claims.

Guilherme, M. (2017). Freire's philosophical contribution for a theory of intercultural ethics: A deductive analysis of his work. *Journal of Moral Education, 46*(4), 422–434.

Haapakoski, J., & Pashby, K. (2017). Implications for equity and diversity of increasing international student numbers in European universities: Policies and practice in four national contexts. *Policy Futures in Education, 15*(3), 360–379.

Harvey, L. (2006). 'Understanding quality', Section B 4.1-1 of 'Introducing Bologna objectives and tools'. In E. Froment, J. Kohler, L. Pursuer, & L. Wilson (Eds.), *EUA Bologna handbook: Making Bologna work.* Brussels and Berlin: European University Association and Raabe.

Harvey, L., & Green, D. (1993). Defining quality. *Assessment & Evaluation in Higher Education, 18*(1), 9–34.

Hayes, A. (2019). 'We loved it because we felt that we existed there in the classroom!': International students as epistemic equals versus double-country oppression. *Journal of Studies in International Education.* https://doi.org/10.1177/1028315319826304.

Hazelkorn, E. (2015). *Rankings and the reshaping of higher education: The battle for world-class excellence.* London: Springer.

Hooks, B. (2014). *Teaching to transgress.* London: Routledge.

Kerr, C. (2001). *The uses of the university.* Harvard: Harvard University Press.

Khan, A., & Gabriel, J. (2018). Resisting the binary divide in higher education: The role of critical pedagogy. *Journal for Critical Education Policy Studies (JCEPS), 16*(1), 30–58.

Klein, S., Benjamin, R., Shavelson, R., & Bolus, R. (2007). The collegiate learning assessment: Facts and fantasies. *Evaluation Review, 31*(5), 415–439.

Lichan, X. (2015). Transitional challenges faced by post-secondary international students and approaches for their successful inclusion in classrooms. *International Journal for Leadership in Learning, 1*(3), 1–28.

Madge, C., Raghuram, P., & Noxolo, P. (2009). Engaged pedagogy and responsibility: A postcolonial analysis of international students. *Geoforum, 40*(1), 34–45.

Marginson, S. (2013). Equals or others? Mobile students in a nationally bordered world. In S. Sovic & M. Blythman (Eds.), *International students negotiating higher education* (pp. 9–27). London: Routledge.

Marginson, S. (2018, April). *The new geopolitics of higher education: Global co-operation, national competition and social inequality in the world-class university sector* (Centre for Global Higher Education (CGHE) Working Paper Series, Paper No. 34).

Mok, K. H. (2017). *Managing international connectivity, diversity of learning and changing labour markets.* London: Springer.

Morgan, J. (2015, July 9). Poor students' 'cognitive gain' may play role in TEF. *Times Higher Education*, pp. 6–7. Accessed on 12 July 2018. Retrieved from https://www.timeshighereducation.com/news/teaching-excellence-framework-poor-students-cognitive-gain-may-play-role.

Roets, G., Vandenabeele, J., & Bouverne-De Bie, M. (2012). Acknowledging ambivalence in a multicultural neighbourhood: In search of an educational space in narrative practices. *International Journal of Lifelong Education, 31*(1), 33–45.

Slaughter, S., & Leslie, L. L. (1997). *Academic capitalism: Politics, policies, and the entrepreneurial university.* Baltimore: The Johns Hopkins University Press.

Tange, H., & Kastberg, P. (2013). Coming to terms with "double knowing": An inclusive approach to international education. *International Journal of Inclusive Education, 17*(1), 1–14.

Tran, L. T., & Vu, T. T. P. (2017). 'Responsibility in mobility': International students and social responsibility. *Globalisation, Societies and Education, 15*(5), 561–575.

Ursin, J. (2015). Finnish experiences of OECD's international assessment of higher education learning outcomes (AHELO). *Hungarian Educational Research Journal, 5*(3), 18–25.

5

Opportunities the TEF Can Offer

This chapter draws on theoretical ideas developed in Chapters 3 and 4 and focuses on opportunities the TEF could offer to help universities create commitment to just, fair and free from coloniality education experiences for international students. Firstly, the chapter critiques the role of politicised priorities that have driven the present shape of the TEF. It then uses this critique to rationalise the need for reconceptualisation of the outcomes the exercise measures. The final section of this chapter lays out the differences between the new outcomes that the book proposes and the current ones and argues that these differences can be significant in prompting epistemic inclusion of international students. The discussion below specifically critiques the role of politically self-centred priorities that have driven developments in the TEF in creating barriers to this inclusion. The chapter also deconstructs the influence of isomorphic marketised pressures on the TEF which, in turn, are seen to influence universities to fall in step with measurements of teaching excellence that do not consider epistemic democracy as one of its determinants. One of the key arguments developed in this chapter is that these pressures are preventing more 'humane' understandings and practice of internationalisation which, in turn, contributes to unequal

© The Author(s) 2019
A. Hayes, *Inclusion, Epistemic Democracy and International Students*,
https://doi.org/10.1007/978-3-030-11401-5_5

105

treatment of international students and their intellectual subordination in university classrooms. It is argued below that these pressures are also the main reason why international students have been mainly left out in any discussions about the TEF, and when they are mentioned, it is always in the context whereby the TEF is represented to help to 'repair' international students' deficits and to increase market competitiveness of the British education system.

The publication of the Green Paper '*Fulfilling Our Potential: Teaching Excellence, Social Mobility and Student Choice*' on 6 November 2015 confirmed the introduction of the TEF (BIS 2015). The exercise was thought to signal one of the biggest changes in UK's higher education, transforming the ways of evaluating the sector from criteria related mainly to research outputs to metrics focusing on teaching excellence, learning environment, learning gain and student outcomes (ibid.). Jo Johnson, then the Minister of State for Universities and Science, justified the need for the TEF in the following way:

> It will identify and incentivise the highest quality teaching to drive up standards in higher education, deliver better quality for students and employers and better value for taxpayers. Our aim is to: place a spotlight on teaching and encourage excellent teaching for all students; help institutions improve the quality of their teaching by highlighting exemplary practices; build a culture where it is recognised that teaching has equal status with research within and across HE institutions (…); support and where possible stimulate the sector to help students meet their aspirations (…); help employers to identify and recruit graduates with the skills they require (…); recognise those institutions that do the most to welcome students from a range of disadvantaged backgrounds; (…) reflect the strength that comes from the diversity of our higher education sector and be flexible in recognising different types of excellence; demonstrate that the quality of higher education is a priority in our country(…) (BIS 2015, pp. 18–19)

Subsequent media analyses of the TEF, for instance, in *Times Higher Education* (Grove 2015) offered quite an extensive examination of the planned TEF metrics, exploring questions about whether these metrics could actually measure the stated commitment to teaching quality and

5 Opportunities the TEF Can Offer   107

to put greater spotlight on teaching (e.g. Franco-Santos and Otley 2017, writing for *The Guardian*). Various parts of the *Times Higher* article read:

> (...) the TEF would root out bad teaching and provide incentives to make good teaching even better. The framework should be informed by a clear set of outcome-focused criteria and metrics. (...) Data indicating how hard an institution's students work outside class could also be relevant to the TEF. Information showing the prevalence of formal teaching qualifications among an institutions academic staff may also provide an insight into the value placed on teaching. (Grove 2015, p. i)

Outlining the plans for the most suitable TEF metrics which could capture the outcomes outlined in the quote above, the article made references to Graham Gibbs's indicators of teaching quality in higher education such as 'various measures of class size, teaching staff, the effort students make and the quality of feedback they receive' (Grove 2015, p. i). The most recent reforms in the US aiming to rank universities in terms of the value for money, graduation rates and employability were also considered. These were thought to be 'easy to use tools that will give students more data than ever before to compare tuition fees and outcomes' (ibid., p. i). It is however surprising that, under the TEF commitment to recognise institutions that do the most to welcome students from diverse backgrounds and to reflect the strength that comes from this diversity, ways of developing a culture that is more inclusive of international students have been left out in any discussions about the TEF.

As of today, the TEF metrics do not 'measure' any aspects of higher education teaching that could be considered to be in any way linked to epistemic inclusion of international students. The current metrics are said by the creators of the TEF to focus on three areas of (a) teaching quality, (b) learning environment, as well as (c) student outcomes and learning gain, yet no references to realisation of international students as epistemic equals are included. Each of these three areas is assessed via core and split metrics, additionally including qualitative evidence submitted by individual providers, known as 'provider submission'. Core metrics include National Satisfaction Survey (NSS) scores (on questions related to teaching, assessment, feedback, and academic support), student continuation rates (based on information submitted to Higher Education Statistics Agency [HESA] and Individualised Learner Records [ILR]), as well as employment and destinations of graduates data provided by Destination of Leavers from Higher Education (DLHE) survey. Split metrics are 'core metrics split into sub-groups reflecting widening participation priorities' (DfE 2018, p. 9). They include categories such as age (to account for scores from mature students), disadvantage (based on the index of multiple deprivation [IMD]—to control for characteristics of students coming from economically and socially deprived areas) and, for instance, disability and ethnicity (as self-declared on HESA and ILR records—to 'measure' the level of support for BAME and disabled students).

The split metrics do in fact include categories of student *domicile* (UK, other EU and non-EU students) identified based on HESA/ILR student self-declarations and applied to NSS scores only. But as the book argues, this 'split' is not sufficient to prompt inclusion of international students as epistemic equals. The book provides a separate discussion of the implications of this split for prompting universities to develop more critical relationships with international students in Part III, but here it is important to note that whilst the split may be seen as the first step towards recognising the impact of international students on higher education, the split means very little in terms of addressing problems of persistent intellectual subordination of international students. Arguably, the split may in fact further amplify this subordination as unsatisfactory performance on split categories in some areas measured by the NSS is likely to be seen to be linked to the perceived cultural and educational gap between international students and the British system. This may in turn perpetuate views that international students are 'inferior' and in need of 'fixing'.

Finally, the qualitative provider submission that is also part of the TEF is intended to provide self-assessed evidence, written by the provider about their learning environment, detailing aspects of 'teaching that provides an appropriate level of contact, stimulation and challenge, and which encourages student engagement and effort (DfE 2017, p. 24). This book argues that the provider's statement could in many ways be used to complement the statistical analysis of the quantitative metrics that are proposed, as it could be a critical space for universities to provide information about how tutors facilitate intercultural dynamism in their classroom. But it is vital, in the first instance, that the TEF has a quantitative (core) metric that measures universities' commitment to intellectual equality of all 'knowers' in the classroom because, as explained in Chapter 1, to change the learning environment, a metric that measures how universities practise plurality of knowledge *has to be part of the system*. It is vital to have such a core metric because 'intercultural education [understood here in terms of epistemic democracy] does not just happen and intercultural skills do not just emerge – they each need to be nurtured and developed' (Spencer-Oatey and Dauber 2015, p. 9). Presently, referents that guide the qualitative provider's submission do not even require universities to comment on such skills.

As student voices are also encouraged to be included in the provider's submission (DfE 2017), the submission could be a unique opportunity to give international students a political voice. Chapter 1 has argued that routine normalisation of international students' voices under national perspectives in the classroom goes unnoticed because these voices do not have the 'backing' from the political power. It has also been emphasised in Chapter 1 that lack of policy requirements to address the problem of such tacit marginalisation may be contributing to unwillingness at universities to do something about it, as educators become socialised and governed by only those 'problems' with internationalisation and international students that are represented in policy. As Chapter 2 has shown, in the UK, these 'problems' are mainly linked to maintaining high levels of recruitment and flows of additional income. Thus, considering student submissions in the provider statement, including information about whether and to what extent international students' experience discrimination in the classroom, and then requiring universities to write a response, to which universities would be held accountable, should be mandated by policy. Only then, universities will be able to prevent such issues from going unnoticed.

Commentators have not shied away from criticising the TEF. Most critiques have focused on the lack of validity of its metrics to measure anything to do with teaching and for having little to do with the actual teaching excellence (e.g. Rust 2017; Gibbs 2017; Race 2017).

As already indicated throughout this book, there are many definitions of teaching excellence, with most analyses agreeing that the difference in definitions can be primarily attributed to varying understandings of 'what higher education is for' (e.g. Skelton 2009; De Courcy 2015; Gourlay and Stevenson 2017). Arguably, however, it would at the same time be safe to assume that, at a time of increased internationalisation of our universities, teaching excellence should also be understood from the perspective of internationalisation—that is, in the sense of universities' skilful engagement in new social and educational interdependencies with international people (here mainly students) and their leadership, through critical pedagogies, in creating social changes that accept these people as epistemic equals. There is little doubt that such understandings of internationalisation would be contested as a valid determinant of teaching excellence as engaging, on equal and reciprocal terms with the myriad of intellectual traditions that can enrich host communities is a skill that only excellent teachers have.

In the meantime, however, discussions about the TEF continue to focus on the invalidity of the 'technical' design of the exercise. NSS questions, for instance, have been said not to be an adequate proxy for teaching because they are heavily influenced by non-academic factors, which include the sex or ethnicity of a lecturer (Grove 2017). Another metric widely contested in various discussions about the TEF is the earnings and destination of leavers data. These have been described by a senior academic as 'completely ludicrous (…) because no allowance is made for the inputs, not only teaching quality but also socio-economic background and the school attended' (cited in Grove 2015, p. i). The earnings data have also been criticised for being used to justify the smaller amounts of public subsidies being awarded to universities whose graduates do not earn much money (Morgan 2016). Of course, it is needless to say that applying the earnings metric to international students would be highly flawed, as the context of employment in their own countries could reveal significant differences in earnings between British and international students for doing the same job. This would naturally affect the credibility of such results going into the TEF. But the wider problem of the absence of metrics and discussions regarding the subordinated status of international students in the classroom is still ignored. The technical aspects of the TEF are of course important because the present metrics still need to produce valid measures of the outcomes they are set to measure (however unrelated to teaching they may be!) What is also important, however, is that the government should also try to measure, through the TEF, different outcomes—ones that are related to internationalisation understood as a process of engagement with intellectual traditions rooted in epistemologies and ontologies of international students. This is important, given that UK, and other universities worldwide, operate in an education space where the mobility of students changes the national character of 'knowing' within higher education.

It is therefore important to scrutinise the TEF in terms of the wider approaches and processes the exercise proposes to use to 'measure' teaching excellence. There are ways in which it is possible to see how monitoring (and incentivising!) better teaching performance of universities through the TEF is linked to competition undercurrents which hold rankings performance as the main gateway to success. It has already been noted elsewhere that 'the TEF operates on the basis that teaching and learning performance can be measured in a simple and straightforward way' (Franco-Santos and Otley 2017). This is seen to be reflected in the TEF metrics focusing on benchmarks and outcomes that already exist and ones that can be measured independently of the influence of the teaching process on them. This last point has specific implications for the metrics on epistemic democracy proposed in this book and the outcomes that the exercise could, but presently does not, measure. The current shape of the TEF metrics enables universities to strategically invest in resources that support 'game playing' and 'working out the system', in order to build up better rankings performance. 'Game playing' subsequently leads to misunderstandings and institutional misarticulations of internationalisation, not requiring universities to work towards social changes which could lead to accepting international people as epistemic equals. The current metrics do not 'measure' such changes as they are not focused on assessing the education process.

The proposed metric in this book (Part III) should not however be merged under the same approaches and processes that drive the current design of the TEF but should instead be seen as an opportunity to start a change that will enable the exercise to assess the *actual* education process. If internationalisation, understood from the perspective of epistemic democracy, were indeed to become part of the TEF, the referents underlying the proposed metric would have to change from its current form (based on structural measurements) including international-home student and staff ratios and numbers of internationally co-authored research papers [see for example *Times Higher Education* rankings], to ones that focus on educational experiences of international students and how they are shaped by conditions of full reciprocity, respect and intellectual equality. However, if the commercial outlook on internationalisation continues to be reinforced through the TEF, universities are then likely to continue to 'ignore' engagement with international students on more democratic terms. This will have consequences not only for the realisation of students as respected and equally qualified members of the classroom community but will also lead to limited constructions and understandings of what teaching excellence is.

So far, any references to international students in the TEF have however suggested a strong influence of the marketised undercurrents on the exercise, reflecting institutional self-interests, expressed in the fear about losing potentially high numbers of international students. Those who have already commented on the possible implications of the changing trends in international students recruitment stated that rating only some universities in the TEF as excellent 'could undermine London as global student hub' (Bothwell 2017). The former head of the University of Oxford, for instance, stated that 'our competitors will be licking their lips that we will start declaring that some institutions are better or worse at teaching than others' (cited in Grove 2015, p. i). These comments reflect the commercial priorities that shape current misunderstandings of internationalisation at universities, additionally suggesting little hope that the TEF will eventually be seen as a vehicle towards greater epistemic inclusion of international students. For the time being, it seems that the TEF will rather remain a vehicle for realisation of politicised objectives of enhancing higher education exports.

Further reading of the TEF also suggests that there are even more reasons to think that international students are likely to be thought of by the government mostly in commercial terms. The discordant trends emerging from the analysis of the scope of the TEF metrics related to diversity suggest that international students are not even considered as 'real people'. This analysis contradicts the government's commitment to represent all groups in the TEF and to encompass the strength that comes from the diversity of higher education (BIS 2015). The first Green Paper states that the TEF will measure excellence that will 'incorporate and reflect the diversity of the sector' and take into account the fact that 'perceptions of excellence vary between students, institutions and employers' (BIS 2015, p. 21). Further analysis of the paper seems to however imply that the TEF is likely to focus only on the diversity that is 'nationally bounded' and 'nationally useful', in the sense of fulfilling self-centered political goals, as the exercises' main focus, especially in terms of value added from higher education, is on those groups that are politically relevant. These groups presently include the disadvantaged and under-represented groups of nationals that enter higher education through widening participation (WP) routes, as these groups are directly associated with the UK's government politicised agenda to increase access to higher education for all (Hayes 2017).

Jo Johnson, the creator of the TEF, and the former Minister for Universities and Science, said, when laying plans for the TEF, that 'one of the core metrics we envisage using in the TEF will be the progress and the value add for students from disadvantaged backgrounds (cited in Havergal 2015). Thus, it is possible to see how plans for such metrics could have been politically motivated because, as commented by some analysts, the inclusion of students from disadvantaged backgrounds in the TEF was motivated by "ministers" drive to meet targets set by the prime minister and a fear of dropout rates rising after the scraping of student number controls' (Morgan 2015, p. 6). But there is also a wider problem here which prompts ethical questions about why similar objectives of the 'value added' and concentrating on the journey travelled by international students have never even been on the agenda?

The answer to this question could be explained by Simon Marginson's (2013) theorisations about ways in which lack of national 'boundedness' excludes international students from the same social, political and educational commitment that the home students receive from national governments. As the international students are not 'bound' to national higher education goals in the same way as, for instance, the WP students mentioned above may be, neither through politically motivated initiatives advocating their increased participation nor their citizenship status, it could be argued that this might be the reason why the creators of the TEF do not place equal emphasis on the experiences of international students. The lack of citizenship status, and its associated representation of British higher education system as an asset for non-citizens (as the general perception is that international students want to arrive in Britain to experience better education), may contribute to constructions of international students as beneficiaries and supplicants of this system (Marginson 2015). This in turn legitimises perceptions that it is their responsibility to do well (in the end they benefit from being here), which release the government from any responsibilities to create conditions for their inclusion as equals. Assumptions about such superiority can be seen in the TEF Green Paper, through statements such as 'England's world-class higher education system is open to anyone with the potential to benefit from it' (BIS 2015, p. 36). This statement is however automatically underpinned by caution that 'not all students will achieve their best within the same model of teaching' (p. 21). That is why those students need to 'receive effective support in order to achieve their educational goals and potential' (p. 33). It is not difficult to see how such discourses can legitimise perceptions that international students are inferior, rather than equal.

Similar discourses can also be noted in the white paper '*Success as a Knowledge Economy: Teaching Excellence, Social Mobility and Student Choice*' (BIS 2016), which was published in May 2016, following the release of the Green Paper discussed above. There are sections of the White Paper suggesting superior and presumptuous (as well as commercialised) attitudes towards international students, which are revealed in declarations that the government will 'continue to meet the needs of international students *who increasingly demand access to top quality higher education*, and help contribute towards boosting education exports' (BIS 2016, p. 9). Meeting the perceived needs of international students is necessary, as the discourse of the white paper continues, because the government recognises that 'our higher education system is internationally renowned, something that is reflected by the high number of students who wish to come here to study' (p. 32). Such problematisations of international students as 'supplicants' therefore prompt policy objectives to offer language and remedial support which, while having some legitimacy, simultaneously reinforce representations of international students as 'deficient'. Under the influence of such policy discourses, these students will therefore never be perceived as intellectually equal.

Remedial support, whilst, on the one hand, being well meaning, on the other, as noted by Marginson (2013), seems to bear implications for one- directional change that burdens international students with the responsibility to adapt, not vice versa. Research, however, has continually shown that international students are active agents that are able to resolve problems stemming from change via institutional behaviours that are 'resourceful'—in the sense of not being assimilationist, because students strategically combine selective elements of what they know about teaching and learning and the newly acquired practices (Brown and Graham 2009; Sovic and Blythman 2013; Ozer 2015). They are a distinctive group of learners that interpret their education experiences through lenses of their previously acquired identities combined with present constructions of learning (e.g. Gu et al. 2010). These characteristics should be treated as an asset, not as a deficit, and ones that can also bring about benefits for home students, especially for those who cannot travel abroad and experience intercultural learning beyond the walls of their university classrooms. But applying a set of metrics in the TEF that are driven by commercial benefits puts a blindfold over the government's eyes which prevents the ministers, and consequently home students as well, from seeing the benefits that arise from mobility of students. As already alluded to throughout this book, influenced by policy discourses that question the intellectual value of international students beyond economic benefits, home students lack agency to engage with their international peers on politically, socially and educationally equal terms. Through that they deny international students' rights to equivalence and continue to position them as unimportant 'other'.

It is therefore not enough to give international students some equivalence in the TEF through including them under the Competition and Markets Authority (CMA) regulations (as the present shape of the TEF does). Inclusion of international students through the CMA continues to position them as commercial objects. The Green Paper states that 'the system needs to reflect the reality of today's higher education sector where the majority of funding for course costs flows from students' (p. 14). It continues to explain that for this reason the government proposes 'to transform the regulatory landscape to put students at its heart' (p. 14), committing itself to applying CMA regulatory guidance, which is a consumer protection law that covers *all* students in cases of fraudulent information regarding their courses, as well as costs and conditions of study. While this may help to ensure better value for money for international students, and in some respects more security, the undercurrents of this strategy are still mainly commercial, carrying no implications for social changes that are required to start accepting international people as equally qualified 'knowers'. Further reading of the Green Paper also suggests that compliance with the consumer law is required to 'safeguard the strong international reputation for English providers' (p. 57) because 'information about the quality of teaching is vital to UK productivity' (p. 19). So it is still *never* about the international students per se. Including them under the CMA rather reveals interest convergence and a situation whereby something is done for international students only if it also brings benefits for the sector.

Indeed, international students seem to be discussed in the Green Paper only insofar there is a high level of 'convergence' between what is being done for them and the reputation of the UK. The government highlights that information about the quality of teaching in the TEF is increasingly important in the globalized world, not because it can give potential overseas candidates information about levels of engagement with international students' identities, but because it will 'guarantee the highest returns (…) and the TEF will offer significant reputational advantage and help recruit students from both home and internationally' (BIS 2015, p. 29). Otherwise, there is no explicit discussion of the potentially subordinated situation of international students that the Green and White papers may create, ignoring moral and ethical questions of how the whole TEF exercise silences the need for more critical relationships with them.

'Un-Silencing' Moral and Ethical Questions About Inclusion of International Students Through the TEF

This section discusses the theoretical basis for creating TEF metrics that could prompt more critical relationships with international students. Based on the arguments above, positing that being largely influenced by marketisation and commercially-driven priorities, the current TEF metrics deny international students equal intellectual rights in the classroom, this section argues that to protect international students from the consequences of reputational and competition driven undercurrents, there has to be a conceptual shift in thinking about what the TEF metrics should actually measure. This shift is the first step in creating measurement outcomes for the TEF concerning internationalisation understood as epistemic democracy, which would be different from the nature and scope of the current assessments in that they would not be focused on outcomes that already exist but would rather evaluate the role of educational processes at universities in creating conditions for equivalence of international students.

In light of the discussion provided in this book so far, it seems logical to suggest that the TEF needs to be about encouraging systemic and moral improvement. Chapter 2 has suggested ways in which it is possible to see how attitudes towards international students as economic objects and as people in educational deficit have historical roots. These representations can be traced back to the strategies for the creation of the British Empire that encouraged expansion of education, positioning international students as "outsiders" that needed to be "enlightened" through education in the prestigious English education system. These attitudes have been sustained in the politics of successive governments, prompting policy objectives increasingly highlighting that international students are strategically important to British education exports and when they are actually in the UK, their deficits need to be corrected. Yes, it is true that some international students indeed need some support in terms of coping with the demands of study but let us not forget, to use Marginson's (2015) words, that they do not arrive in England 'to be more English than the English'. Rather, as Chapter 1 has shown, they come here with full expectations that their unique perspectives, learning behaviours and ethnic and cultural identities will be respected. The previous sections of this chapter have additionally shown that when these historic influences are coupled with commercial and reputational priorities, that seem to have driven the very idea of the TEF, as well as its subsequent developments, it is time to think how education policy can advocate for international students' voice as equal and how it can place this voice to drive critical pedagogical engagement with global and home students in the classroom. This requires thinking about what the TEF should *additionally* (or perhaps even *instead*) be assessing.

The short answer to this question is that it should be assessing the *education process* (Gibbs 2010). It is also important that this process is assessed through metrics that will not perpetuate the 'problems' other national rankings have created—i.e. enabling universities to play political games and to reinforce structural measurements, especially those related to internationalisation, which, overall, have little emancipatory value for the students. Structural measurements never focus on how educational processes can prompt specific outcomes (here these would mean intellectual equivalence of international perspectives in the classroom) but instead prevent democratic ideas that could make a genuine difference to the students. As Pascarella (2001) has argued:

> [A] serious problem with national rankings is that from a research point of view, they are largely invalid. That is, they are based on institutional resources and reputational dimensions which have only minimal relevance to what we know about the impact of college on students (...). But, as has often been said, the academy has the unfortunate tendency to apply scientific standards of evidence to every field of study except itself (...) Institutional leaders actually reinforce the credibility of the national magazine rankings, and do their own schools a disservice, when they promulgate policies directed at improving their institution's yearly rank in the queue, instead of focusing on improving the educational experiences that make a genuine difference for their students. (Pascarella 2001, pp. 20–21)

The fact that variables and predictors used in various commercialised rankings, and especially those related to internationalisation, do not actually explain what a university *does* with or for international students, should be a sufficient reason to re-think the current scope and nature of metrics on internationalisation. The direction of change in these rankings should be towards the type of difference which, as described by Pascarella, is related to improvements in students' experience caused by the *actual* educational processes. University rankings should therefore focus on the quality of teaching measured through assessing the scope and nature of interactions between students and staff, reciprocal engagement between home and international students and the degree to which this engagement in engineered by university tutors. These are the dimensions of university performance that are much more important in defining what a university does in terms of realisation of international students as epistemic equals, than structural factors of international-home students ratios or internationally co-authored research. And only when such dimensions are measured through official rankings such as the TEF, the creators of the exercise can talk about attempting to define teaching excellence in higher education.

A striking lack of realisation that the present shape of the TEF can cause damaging effects for international students emerges through the analysis of the current, structurally-focused metrics. These do not help anybody to understand the relationship between pedagogies, curriculum context and international students experiences of exclusion. In fact, what the government keeps doing is to continue to commission inquiries about the value of international students, as if this value needs to be continually proved, which further alienate these learners as they re-inforce the view that there is 'something wrong' with international students. Any such inquiry automatically assumes and sends a public message that there is a degree of scepticism about the value of international students in higher education. In the recent inquiry, for instance, commissioned by the Home Office and administered by the Migration Advisory Committee (MAC) the value of international students has been questioned based on the perceived effects international students have on the education experiences of home students. The opening section to the survey read as follows:

120   A. Hayes

> The independent Migration Advisory Committee (MAC) has been asked by the Government to evaluate the impact of international students in the UK. To help them do this, they would like to gain a better understanding of your time as a student and the *impacts* that international students have had on it. By participating in this survey, you will have made your experiences heard, and are helping shape the evidence and recommendations that will be put forward to Government.

The ways in which MAC has tried to gain a better understanding of the impact of international students on home students' experiences unfortunately include attitudinal questions requiring the students to indicate whether they are 'impacted' (socially and educationally) positively or negatively by the presence of international students. The opening statement also encourages participants to take part in the survey as an opportunity for their voices to be heard, suggesting a narrative that 'if you feel you have been negatively affected by international students, now it's your chance to say it!'. It is possible to see how such a survey can encourage divisive attitudes, especially that subsequent questions also ask respondents to indicate how likely they are to continue interactions and friendships with international students beyond the current context of education (where they have to do it, as opposed to informal settings where there is no obligation to do so). It is clear how such questions are fulfilling political goals related to decisions about post-study work visas and other international students controls, having little to do with any potential shift in representations of international students as equally qualified participants in the education process. Rather, it seems that the survey attempts to assess how much of a 'nuisance' international students are for home students, positioning home students as central. Through such positioning equivalence of international students looks very unlikely.

The survey has now been withdrawn but it has raised yet another alarm about its influence in shaping derogatory representations of international students. Why is nobody asking how international students experience interactions with home students and whether their universities actually do anything about it? Such questions would be likely to change their position from 'inferior' to 'equal' and would additionally

5 Opportunities the TEF Can Offer 121

challenge the current starting position of the survey which highlights that there are 'other' in the UK education system and that home students are central. It is argued in this book that the TEF could challenge the negative effects such surveys could create, for both international and home students. For the former, through the metrics that are proposed in Part III, the exercise could create conditions for epistemic inclusion, for the latter, it could highlight that the presence of international students is a unique opportunity for their wider development. Above all, the proposed TEF metrics would also evaluate the role of the educational process in creating more emancipatory attitudes towards international students, freeing them from controls and scrutinising processes that presently do not appreciate that being able to give international students greater agency is a dimension of high quality teaching and excellence in higher education.

Such TEF effects will however not be achieved if the current metrics stay the same. They need to therefore be re-shifted to include 'measures of the educational process' (Gibbs 2010, p. 2). In the context of this book, this means evaluating how through complimentary positioning of international and home students as 'experts', university tutors can represent both groups as 'equals'. This would require processes of democratisation which could be initiated through pedagogies that provide a forum for sharing cultural knowledge in ways that acknowledge relationalities between home and global perspectives, instead of, as indicated in relation to the MAC survey, merely assessing whether the impact of the latter is positive or negative for home students. The latter are likely to position home perspectives as normative, suggesting that the host community should remain unchanged and 'unmoved' by the presence of international people. Such positioning, as explained in Chapter 4, is against the key principles of Freire's critical pedagogy which is based on the idea that the oppressed are not 'marginals', nor should they be encouraged to replace the oppressors. Rather, they need to be 'inside the structure which makes them beings for others' (Freire 1970, p. 74).

As the preparations for revisions to the TEF are taking place within the context of nationally stagnated attitudes towards international students, the TEF needs to actively seek to include metrics that will prompt greater commitment to plurality in our universities. The TEF should aim to assess a mode of teaching and forms of curriculum content that engage equally with all student identities in one common setting, reflecting through such assessments greater progress in terms of their cosmopolitan development (Rizvi 2009). The latest evidence from the International Students' Survey (QS Solutions 2018) clearly suggests that international students are looking to see evidence of such development in the TEF results. The survey has shown that international students want to see TEF ratings that reveal how universities support international students' experience. Such metrics are seen by international students as an indication of how welcoming UK universities are. Additionally, in the context of looking for value for money, international students also seek to understand how the TEF can represent levels of international students' satisfaction with their courses and teaching quality (QS Solutions 2018). In short, it seems that they would like to see *their* experiences being put on par with those of home students. The model proposed in Part III of this book offers opportunities to give international students the equal status that they seem to be seeking through the TEF, and to consider their experiences as worthy of equal consideration. It is important therefore to understand the conceptual underpinnings of this model (which are explained below), to reveal ways in which the model differs from the nature and scope of the existing TEF metrics and how through these differences it can prompt epistemic inclusion of international students.

The key conceptual idea of the model is that it is not intended to measure any hard educational outcomes (such as for example, grades or degree classification), nor it is predicated on student previous achievements or educational backgrounds—not least in the sense of how much student grades count before joining university, for instance, or in the sense of the extent to which the nature of their pre-higher education educational and social experiences can predict their success and experiences at university. Yes, international students' unique backgrounds, as well as educational and cultural identities are conceptually relevant for the model, but not as predictors of their university performance but rather as a source of getting to terms with 'double-knowing'. The current problem with the TEF is that metrics incorporating elements of students' backgrounds are presently used to calculate various sorts of performance indicators for universities—i.e. how well universities can do, considering the type of students they get. Through such focus, they exclude any assessments of whether these backgrounds are taken into account in teaching and learning processes, and whether they have influenced social changes in university classrooms that accept 'foreigners' as intellectual equals. So, the proposed model is intended to measure the cosmopolitan ways of university classrooms, whereby greater equivalence of perspectives beyond the British state is emphasised with the view to developing ways of learning and teaching that are based on mutually respectful interactions between home and international learners. By distancing the proposed model from hard outcomes, and instead focusing on the educational processes per se, the book aims to prompt ideas for a TEF metric that can encourage a more progressive engagement with international students. This engagement would *not* be based on 'highly entrenched traditions of educational policies and practices that remain largely locally defined' (Rizvi 2009, p. 263). Rather, it would represent transformations in teaching that acknowledge the relationalities that surround changes in host communities which have become more hybrid through their interconnectedness with global people (Rizvi 2009).

The proposed model therefore characterises what is going on in teaching and learning in terms of pedagogical processes and includes assessments of consequences of what is going on for how students feel about themselves as 'equals'. The 'variables' that are therefore included in the model concern a specific range of inclusive pedagogical practices that engender reciprocal student engagement (in the sense of giving equal agency to home and international students, encouraging to express everybody's views and values in non-derogatory ways and practising skills in developing understanding of 'knowledges' of people from diverse backgrounds). And while 'engagement' has been a problematic concept related to learning in higher education, not least because of difficulties in defining it (Kahu and Nelson 2018), but also, for instance, because commercialisation of higher education shapes understandings of engagement that emphasise accountability through performativity (Barnacle and Dall'Alba 2017), it has at the same time been found to be the most reliable and reasonable indicator of teaching quality associated with some kind of social change in the classroom (e.g. for latest review of the link between engagement and teaching quality, see Leach 2016). It certainly makes sense to use it when teaching excellence and quality are understood from the perspective of internationalisation and epistemic democracy as processes that aim to lead to social changes that accept international people as 'equals'. How else can this change be achieved if not through critical engagement with their knowledges?

In the US, for instance, a number of large scale studies on student engagement have been conducted, examining a wide range of engagement processes variables and their relationship to specific educational gains. These studies have, for instance, shown significant links between student engagement and various outcomes, in terms of hard successes reflected in successfully completing the first year of study (LaNasa et al. 2007), as well as 'softer' gains such as better critical thinking (e.g. Carini et al. 2006). Hence, the National Survey of Student Engagement (NSSE) has been created in the US to show 'how the institution deploys its resources and organises the curriculum and other learning opportunities to get students to participate in activities that decades of research studies show are linked to student learning' (NSSE website). The NSSE has also been used to design UKES which is used as a sample dataset in the proposed TEF model in this book.

A recent analysis of international students' adaptation to higher education has highlighted that faculty's engagement with cultural variation in-class, and students' interest in cross-cultural interaction relates to a better sense of community (Glass et al 2017). This seems to suggest that creating 'the emphasis on international student difference [which] encourages a partial understanding of their participation and plays to a deficit discourse' (Straker 2016, p. 300) should by no means be the way forward. This unfortunately seems to be the way the TEF represents the terms on which engagement with international students should happen, despite widely agreed views that the deficit discourse sets international students apart and can limit their sense of belonging to the institution, creating gaps between internationalisation and opportunities for equality (Sovic 2009; Killick 2017; Jones 2017). Such opportunities, as it is argued in Part III, can however be evoked through the emphasis in the

TEF on critical engagement with international students' intellectual traditions, which can then help to examine its relationality to a range of teaching process variables and to shape an understanding of a specific type of educational gain—one that evokes the overall growth of students in the sense of their greater appreciation of perspectives beyond their own educational traditions. In this sense, this growth has a liberating nature, freeing the oppressed (international students) and the oppressor (home students) from the limiting effects of policies that set only home perspectives as normative. Being free of these effects means having the agency to engage with 'others' as intellectual equals.

Thus, Part III of this book identifies teaching process variables that can be used to 'measure' the type of the growth of students explained above, drawing on selected questionnaire items from UKES. These variables centre around levels of active engagement with diversity, the extent of active and collaborative learning and reciprocity in student-faculty interactions. There is no single dimension of the teaching process that can measure such an extent, which is also why the proposed model offers multilevel analyses that can be used more confidently to interpret how dimensions of teaching interact to create conditions for intellectual appreciation of the 'other'. In other words, the proposed model will enable universities to learn about the 'value added' provided by institutions through assessments of how teachers develop critical appreciation of other people's knowledges and how students themselves *progress as people.*

References

Barnacle, R., & Dall'Alba, G. (2017). Committed to learn: Student engagement and care in higher education. *Higher Education Research and Development, 36*(7), 1326–1338.

BIS (Department for Business, Innovation and Skills). (2015). *Fullfilling our potential: Teaching excellence, social mobility and student choice* (Green Paper, cm 9141). HMG, UK.

BIS (Department for Business, Innovation and Skills). (2016). *Success as a knowledge economy: Teaching excellence, social mobility and student choice* (White Paper, cm 9258). HMG, UK.

Bothwell, E. (2017). TEF: Results 'could undermine' London as global student hub. *Times Higher Education*. Accessed on 25 July 2018. Retrieved from https://www.timeshighereducation.com/news/tef-results-could-undermine-london-global-student-hub.

Brown, L., & Graham, I. (2009). The discovery of the self through the academic sojourn. *Existential Analysis: Journal of The Society for Existential Analysis, 20*(1), 79–93.

Carini, R. M., Kuh, G. D., & Klein, S. P. (2006). Student engagement and student learning: Testing the linkages. *Research in Higher Education, 47*(1), 1–32.

De Courcy, E. (2015). Defining and measuring teaching excellence in higher education in the 21st century. *College Quarterly, 18*(1), i–vi.

DfE (Department for Education). (2017, October). *Teaching excellence and student outcomes framework specification*. Accessed on 25 July 2018. Retrieved from https://www.gov.uk/government/publications/teaching-excellence-and-student-outcomes-framework-specification.

DfE (Department for Education). (2018). *Teaching Excellence and Student Outcomes Framework: Subject-level Consultation document*. Accessed on 02 Mar 2019. Available from https://consult.education.gov.uk/higher-education-reform/teaching-excellence-and-student-outcomes-framework/supporting_documents/Teaching%20Excellence%20and%20Student%20Outcomes%20Framework%20subjectlevel.pdf.

Franco-Santos, M., & Otley, D. (2017). The Tef won't improve teaching—Universities will just play the game. *The Guardian (Higher Education Network)*, published on 22 June 2017. Retrieved from https://www.theguardian.com/higher-education-network/2017/jun/22/the-tef-wont-improve-teaching-universities-will-just-play-the-game.

Freire, P. (1970). *Pedagogy of the oppressed* (M.B. Ramos, Trans.). New York: Continuum (published as Penguin Classics 2017).

Gibbs, G. (2010, September). *Dimensions of quality*. A paper presented for the Higher Education Academy (HEA). Retrieved from https://www.heacademy.ac.uk/system/files/dimensions_of_quality.pdf.

Gibbs, G. (2017). Evidence does not support the rationale of the TEF. *Compass: Journal of Learning and Teaching, 10*(2). Retrieved from https://journals.gre.ac.uk/index.php/compass/issue/view/51.

Glass, C. R., Gesing, P., Hales, A., & Cong, C. (2017). Faculty as bridges to co-curricular engagement and community for first-generation international students. *Studies in Higher Education, 42*(5), 895–910.

Gourlay, L., & Stevenson, J. (2017). Teaching excellence in higher education: Critical perspectives. *Teaching in Higher Education, 22*(4), 391–395.

Grove, J. (2015, July 23). How might a teaching excellence framework be built? *Times Higher Education*. Accessed on 25 July 2018. Retrieved from https://www.timeshighereducation.com/features/teaching-excellence-framework-tef-how-might-it-be-built.

Grove, J. (2017). TEF to limit use of 'flawed' NSS scores. *Times Higher Education*. Accessed on 25 July 2018. Retrieved from https://www.timeshighereducation.com/news/tef-limit-use-flawed-nss-scores.

Gu, Q., Schweisfurth, M., & Day C. (2010). Learning and growing in a foreign culture. *Compare: A Journal of Comparative and International Education, 40*(1), 7–23.

Havergal, C. (2015). Can policy sort the wheat from the chaff? *Times Higher Education, 2229,* 7.

Hayes, A. (2017). Why international students have been "TEF-ed out"? *Educational Review, 69*(2), 218–231.

Jones, E. (2017). Problematising and reimagining the notion of 'international student experience'. *Studies in Higher Education, 42*(5), 933–943.

Kahu, E. R., & Nelson, K. (2018). Student engagement in the educational interface: Understanding the mechanisms of student success. *Higher Education Research & Development, 37*(1), 58–71.

Killick, D. (2017). *Internationalization and diversity in higher education: Implications for teaching, learning and assessment.* London: Palgrave.

LaNasa, S. M., Olson, E., & Alleman, N. (2007). The impact of on-campus student growth on first-year student engagement and success. *Research in Higher Education, 48*(8), 941–966.

Leach, L. (2016). Enhancing student engagement in one institution. *Journal of Further and Higher Education, 40*(1), 23–47.

Marginson, S. (2013). Equals or others? Mobile students in a nationally bordered world. In S. Sovic & M. Blythman (Eds.), *International students negotiating higher education* (pp. 9–27). London: Routledge.

Marginson, S. (2015, July 1–3). *UK international education: Global position and national prospects.* Paper presented at UK Council for International Students Affairs Conference, University of Sussex.

Morgan, J. (2015). Cameron access targets 'a major factor' in higher education Green Paper. *Times Higher Education*. Accessed on 25 July 2018. Retrieved from https://www.timeshighereducation.com/news/cameron-access-targets-major-factor-higher-education-green-paper.

Morgan, J. (2016). Graduate earnings figures with explosive political impact. *Times Higher Education*. Accessed on 25 July 2018. Retrieved from https://www.timeshighereducation.com/blog/graduate-earnings-figures-explosive-political-impact.

Ozer, S. (2015). Predictors of international students' psychological and sociocultural adjustment to the context of reception while studying at Aarhus University, Denmark. *Scandinavian Journal of Psychology, 56*(6), 717–725.

Pascarella, E. T. (2001). Identifying excellence in undergraduate education are we even close? *Change: The Magazine of Higher Learning, 33*(3), 18–23.

QS Enrolment Solutions. (2018). *International students survey*. Accessed on 26 July 2018. Retrieved from https://www.internationalstudentsurvey.com/international-student-survey-2018/.

Race, P. (2017). The Teaching Excellence Framework (TEF): Yet more competition—And on the wrong things! *Compass: Journal of Learning and Teaching, 10*(2). Retrieved from https://journals.gre.ac.uk/index.php/compass/issue/view/51.

Rizvi, F. (2009). Towards cosmopolitan learning. *Discourse: Studies in the Cultural Politics of Education, 30,* 253–268.

Rust, C. I. (2017). The emperor has no clothes. *Compass: Journal of Learning and Teaching, 10*(2). Retrieved from https://journals.gre.ac.uk/index.php/compass/issue/view/51.

Skelton, A. M. (2009). A 'teaching excellence' for the times we live in? *Teaching in Higher Education, 14*(1), 107–112.

Sovic, S. (2009). Hi-bye friends and the herd instinct: International and home students in the creative arts. *Higher Education, 58*(6), 747.

Sovic, S., & Blythman, M. (Eds.). (2013). *International students negotiating higher education: Critical perspectives*. London: Routledge.

Spencer-Oatey, H., & Dauber, D. (2015). *How internationalised is your university?* UKCISA Occasional Paper. Accessed on 26 June 2016. Retrieved from http://institutions.ukcisa.org.uk/Info-for-universities-colleges–schools/Publications–research/resources/84/How-internationalised-is-your-university.

Straker, J. (2016). International student participation in higher education: Changing the focus from "international students" to "participation". *Journal of Studies in International Education, 20*(4), 299–318.

Part III

A TEF Metric on Internationalisation and Epistemic Democracy—How Could it Work?

6

Suitable Data

This chapter begins the practical part of the book by reviewing the nature and scope of data already collected by the higher education sector (nationally in the UK and internationally) and critiquing their 'suitability' for the metric outlined in Chapters 3, 4 and 5. This chapter also conceptualises the nature of the analysis of these data to show what kind of data modelling is required for the proposed metric, in order for the metric to measure outcomes that focus on the extent to which epistemic inclusion of international students is realised through specific characteristics of the teaching process. Conceptualisations of the analysis process in this chapter draw attention to the ways in which the TEF can lead to significant systemic changes.

It would be inadequate to say that national assessment exercises such as the TEF cannot 'measure' levels of reciprocal engagement with international students at universities because the sector does not collect relevant data. It would be a poor excuse not to try to design such measurements. While it is probably true that the data that are presently collected by the higher education sector in England are limited, in that they do not directly ask about relationality between the teaching process and epistemic inclusion, this does not mean that it is impossible

© The Author(s) 2019
A. Hayes, *Inclusion, Epistemic Democracy and International Students*,
https://doi.org/10.1007/978-3-030-11401-5_6

131

to design metrics that can assess whether tutors are working towards democratisation of their relationships with international students by deploying relevant pedagogies. This chapter demonstrates how the limitations of the current data can be overcome by the change in ways they are currently analysed for the TEF, shifting the focus from estimating proxies and benchmarks for universities regarding outcomes that already exit, to focusing the analysis on the extent to which intellectual reciprocity in student and staff relationships changes with the characteristics of the teaching process.

In England, there *are* national sector surveys that could be used to assess this extent. For example, the UK Engagement Survey (UKES) asks questions about the levels of engagement of students in the classroom community and whether students are explicitly encouraged by their courses to be part of this community. UKES questions also ask students to indicate whether their overall course experience encourages them to develop an understanding of people from diverse backgrounds, and whether alongside developing these understandings, the students also have opportunities to develop and clarify their personal views and ethics. Reciprocity that is contained by such questions, which ask about opportunities to learn about others, whilst simultaneously developing own views and ethics, is the basis on which the new metric proposed in this book is developed. If such reciprocity is considered in the TEF, the new metric is likely to invite explorations of complimentary effects of learning about both, home and international students, and how these effects engage both groups of students as 'equals'. It is true of course that UKES does not directly ask about intellectual engagement, but its items (being the only ones that presently ask about engagement) are used in this book to conceptualise the design and operationalisation of the proposed metric, rather than to design a 'perfect' metric, as this would of course require more specific questions about epistemic democracy to be included in the survey. Additionally, the intention of the new metric is not to 'overemphasise' identities of international students, as this could compromise opportunities for reciprocal engagement with all knowledges in the classroom. Rather, the new TEF metric is intended to invite democratically-oriented classroom activism which creates situations in which international and home students can be interchangeably positioned as equally

NSS questions 1 to 4 which cover the NSS scale 'Teaching on my course'. 1 - Staff are good at explaining things. 2 - Staff have made the subject interesting. 3 - Staff are enthusiastic about what they are teaching. 4 - The course is intellectually stimulating.
NSS questions 5 to 9 which cover the NSS scale 'Assessment and Feedback'. 5 - The criteria used in marking have been clear in advance. 6 - Assessment arrangements and marking have been fair. 7 - Feedback on my work has been prompt. 8 - I have received detailed comments on my work. 9 - Feedback on my work has helped me clarify things I did not understand.
NSS questions 10 to 12 which cover the NSS scale "Academic Support". 10 - I have received sufficient advice and support with my studies. 11 - I have been able to contact staff when I needed to. 12 - Good advice was available when I needed to make study choices.

Fig. 6.1 NSS questions constituting part of the TEF metrics—adapted from HEFCE consultation document—http://www.hefce.ac.uk/media/HEFCE,2014/Content/Pubs/2016/201632/HEFCE2016_32a-g.PDF

qualified 'experts'. So far, as argued elsewhere, the current TEF metrics position international students mostly as the 'other' (Hayes 2017).

The National Student Survey (NSS), for example, whose core questions about 'Teaching on my course', 'Assessment and feedback' and 'Academic support' (see Fig. 6.1) presently constitute core TEF metrics, do not make any references to teaching practices that emphasise commitment to plurality. Despite looking at variations in student responses based on the 'split' categories by students' 'domicile' (i.e. between UK, other EU, and non-EU students), the TEF metrics still leave out assessments of the extent to which international students are democratically included in the classroom community. Instead, they merely establish how home and international students fare on the various measures relative to their peers. Whilst there is some insight to be gained about learning about satisfaction levels between home and international students by looking at the 'split' list of the core metrics scores, these tell us nothing about the degree to which the recorded satisfaction levels are associated with participation in classroom activities that are based on attunement to the lives and knowledges of international students.

134   A. Hayes

This book therefore intends to encourage the creators of the TEF to think of ways in which the exercise can appropriate understandings of teaching excellence that, aside 'technical aspects' of good course design, effective feedback and academic support for students, also encompass internationalisation understood as epistemic democracy as one of its key determinants. As explained in Chapter 5, the understanding of internationalisation considered under the TEF should evolve from the growth of universities that enter into new intellectual interdependencies with international students and should therefore include assessments of social changes that accept these people as epistemic equals. If such assessments are included as part of the TEF, they can create *intentions* for such changes at universities and prompt a critical appreciation of their benefits, manifested in emancipation of international students as well as home students gaining more access to intellectual and civic advantages of internationalisation. The proposed TEF metric can create a policy discourse that does not position experiences of home students as 'central', but can rather create a public view that both home and international experiences are 'equal'. The proposed metric can shape a policy 'mantra' that affords knowledge production to *all* people, activating through this their agency and allowing for self-determination, under the aim of producing knowledge. As indicated throughout this book, the meaning of internationalisation the proposed metric is likely to shape makes it a process that is an adaptive response to cross-border people. Through this adaptation, internationalisation can therefore facilitate the production of knowledge and re-shape the philosophical assumptions about learning—that is, that learning does not take place by acquiring normative contents and structures set by nation states but is rather constitutive of global interconnectedness that makes knowledge production an (intended) 'effect' of interactions between worldwide political, economic, social, and cultural 'knowledges'. But to make such knowledge production intentional, universities need a 'plan' and a commonly agreed frame that will create, and then sustain, intentions to construct international students as equal knowledge producers, without whom home students cannot fully benefit from higher education.

'Technically' speaking then, in terms of the kind of data that would be suitable to show such intentions, we would need a TEF metric to contain information about whether university staff practice critical pedagogy, aiming to fight coloniality (as explained in Chapters 3, 4 and 5). Such information is not presently evoked in the TEF. The TEF seems to place a lot of importance on students' satisfaction but ways in which this satisfaction may be related to interactions with other students and staff are not considered. For example, an article in *Times Higher Education,* discussing why the current NSS metrics can be seen as a proxy of excellent teaching, highlighted that 'NSS scores can be relevant because they provide information about whether students are happy or not. (…) They are a proxy for learning gain because students who report better experiences gain better degrees' (Grove 2015, p. i). Better experiences are however not considered in the present NSS metrics in terms of their relationality to teaching on student courses—i.e. how much of student satisfaction with the course can be explained by teaching that treats everybody as 'equal'.

It is also widely known that the relationship between better learning experiences and better degrees does not apply to international students in the same way as it may do to home students. Research has shown that international students often report high satisfaction with their learning experiences because they 'bear the responsibility to persist, overcome their discomfort, and integrate into the host society' (Lee and Rice 2007, p. 388). For fear of being discriminated, not fitting in, and influenced by the perceived superiority of the host country education system, international students do not challenge the host institutions and feel it is their responsibility to adapt (Hayes 2018). Thus, they are more likely to tick the 'highly satisfied boxes' on evaluation tools such as the NSS, reflecting a high degree of the expected compliance rather than genuine satisfaction with their courses. Additionally, even when they *are* genuinely happy with their learning experiences, the fact that there often isn't a linear relationship with high degree classifications and course satisfaction of international students can be explained by the whole range of other factors which may be affecting international students' attitudes towards first class degrees, which may or may not differ from those held by home students. It is important to note that these factors are not at play because international students are 'deficient', which is unfortunately often assumed. Rather, they affect international students because those students need to critically re-balance all the new roles and responsibilities (in educational but also in 'identity' terms) in ways they never had to do before in their countries of origin (Mwale et al. 2018), because the lack of nation-boundedness (in educational, cultural and legal terms) to the country of education denies them access to the same human rights and benefits home students can enjoy more freely (Marginson 2012) and because educational mobility for international students is a specific form of 'becoming' (Tran 2016) which involves decision making that rests on different factors than those prioritised by home students as, arguably, the latter do not have to, for instance, think about securing migration through education in the country of education or re-establishing their social status on return home. In fact, these differences aside, there is also plenty of evidence which suggests that course satisfaction for home students does not mean better educational outcomes either, due to factors reaching far beyond teaching (e.g. Jones et al. 2017).

Thus, for the TEF to reconceptualise understandings of excellent teaching, to make it inclusive of internationalisation as one its determinants, the reporting on student satisfaction levels (as well as other aspects of their classroom experiences) need to change from aggregating scores on, for instance, NSS items and calculating their distance from the university benchmark (z-scores), to finding ways of capturing how student satisfaction levels change with the characteristics of the teaching process. The TEF therefore needs to assess the *relational* nature between student satisfaction with their courses and the contribution teaching that encourages critical engagement with international students makes to this satisfaction. Presently, the current NSS ratings 'split' based on students' domicile merely show how well universities perform in the international and home students category. And whilst this split performance on the NSS is welcome to a certain extent, as the separate category of performance for international students can be seen as the first step towards acknowledging their impact on universities, it is also very divisive as it separates the performance of 'us' and 'them'. Simply looking at the difference in NSS scores for home and international students will not prompt understandings that assessments of excellent teaching should include skills related to how teachers bring 'us' and 'them' together. Without changes to the analysis of the 'split' NSS data, the TEF is likely to further fossilise the inferior status of international students and their representations as commercial objects. For instance, if the performance of universities in the 'split' category for international students is weak, institutions may then be likely to intensify the remedial support for international students as, despite research showing that international students thrive when the freedom to exercise their own agency is enabled by democratising social relations in the classroom (e.g. Spiro 2014), most reactions at universities to unsatisfactory learning experience are still linked to the perceived socio-cultural and academic gaps between international students and their host countries (e.g. Liu and Lin 2016). Conversely, good performance in the 'split' category for international students may be likely to inform their more 'energetic' recruitment. Both reactions are thus likely to perpetuate the same constructions of international students as deficient, and when the performance in the split category exceeds the target for international students, as commercial objects enhancing university rankings performance.

If the TEF was however to prevent such reactions, continuing to use NSS metrics as core indicators, the NSS would have to include additional questions. These questions would have to be focused, in the first instance, on assessing the extent to which unique perspectives and learning behaviours of international students are respected and encouraged in the classroom, but also on emphasising the benefits and opportunities for inter-cultural development that arise from internationalisation. The continued argument in this book is that realisation of international students as epistemic equals should not be understood as 'overemphasising' their identities. Rather, epistemic inclusion of international students should be understood as a new classroom activism which supports learning that evolves under conditions of interchangeable positioning of home and international students as intellectual 'equals'. Only through such positioning both groups of students can interact on reciprocal basis and universities can then explicate the benefits of internationalisation as a process that leads to global imagination of even most locally focused knowledge. Such understanding of internationalisation is currently not measured in official rankings (in the TEF and beyond), as present internationalisation referents rely mostly on countable and structural measures of home-international student ratios, numbers of internationally mobile staff and students, as well as internationally co-authored publications and internationally co-led research projects (Seeber et al. 2016). Such understanding is however needed if excellent teaching in higher education is ever to be considered from the perspective of working towards social change that is inclusive of all students as equally qualified knowers.

The book argues that including UKES data in the TEF may on the other hand help appropriate understandings of teaching excellence that is measured based on criteria related to internationalisation as a responsive process leading to epistemic democracy.

It has already been suggested elsewhere that UKES may be a better proxy for teaching excellence than the NSS because it measures 'learning gain' that is based on levels of engagement rather than levels of satisfaction. The argument ran that one can be happy and not learn much but it is unlikely that one can be engaged and not learn much (Havergal 2015). But again, and similarity to the NSS data, caution needs to be exercised about how UKES responses would need to be analysed. If based on merely aggregating scores on individual UKES items, the TEF may continue to position international students as 'others'. UKES items represent 'British' understandings of engagement in the classroom and position them as normative in the survey. This means that students who do not comply with these understandings (as, for instance, was shown in Chapter 1) can be perceived as 'deficient'. But it is again important to recognise that international students may not engage with their universities in the same way as their home counterparts do. Evidence often suggests that international students' approaches to study are sometimes very pragmatic (and seen in negative terms as being instrumental), for cultural, sponsorship or language difficulty reasons (Malcolm and Mendoza 2014; Oikonomidoy and Williams 2013). This does not however mean that they are not learning. Lack of acknowledgement of this difference however may lead to false assumptions that they are deficient, whereas often international students decide not to engage (in terms defined by the UKES), as their goals are purely practical—i.e. focused on completing a degree and fulfilling the conditions of their sponsorship. To achieve these pragmatic goals, and to balance the additional responsibilities of sponsorship that home students do not have, taking part in critical discussions and engaging in extra-curricular activities is sometimes not seen by international students as necessary (e.g. Toogood 2015). Culturally, for many international students learning 'tangible' or 'usable' knowledge is also more important than, for instance, developing soft skills that some of the UKES items ask about (see Fig. 6.2).

So, it is very important that pragmatism underlying international students' attitudes to study is not mistaken for 'deficiencies'. Simply aggregating scores on UKES items that represent understandings of engagement normalised in the British culture can overlook the complexity of student choices in terms of their engagement, which may again prompt the same reactions at universities as unsatisfactory NSS scores—namely that international students' deficits need to be fixed. The analysis of UKES based on aggregation of scores, therefore, if included under the TEF, will neither prompt understandings of teaching excellence based on internationalisation, nor will it help to challenge subordination of international students already established by, for instance, the NSS and the wider TEF exercise (see Chapter 5). In fact, if the TEF relies on aggregated UKES scores, it will further legitimise this subordination.

During the current academic year, how much has your course emphasised the following activities?
1. Evaluating or judging a point of view, decision or information source
2. Worked with other students on course projects or assignments

During the current academic year, about how often have you done each of the following?
3. Asked questions in taught sessions or contributed to discussions about course material in other ways
4. Connected your learning to real-world problems or issues
5. Examined the strengths and weaknesses of your own views on a topic or issue
6. Tried to better understand someone else's views by imagining how an issue looks from his or her perspective
7. Changed the way you thought about a concept or issue as a result of what you learned
8. Connected ideas from your course to your prior experience and knowledge

---

Fig. 6.2 Sample soft skills evaluated by UKES that may not be applicable to international students for reasons explained above, adapted from 2017 UKES Questionnaire

But as already alluded to in Chapter 5, the focus on 'engagement' in UKES, however, offers a potential for a TEF metric that can help to expedite understandings of excellent teaching which includes internationalisation and epistemic democracy (beyond structural referents mentioned above) as one of its determinants. There are items in the UKES survey that focus on reciprocal relationships between students and staff, and they are really the cornerstone of the proposed metric. An adequate analysis of these items can show how such relationships can lead to inclusion of international students as epistemic equals and that there are developmental benefits of this inclusion for home students as well. The TEF can therefore unlock new social and educational interdependencies with international students and show whether universities undergo social changes that accept these students as epistemic equals. The UKES items that should be selected for TEF metrics to create this understanding are listed in Chapter 7. Chapter 7 also provides details of the statistical analysis of these items. But first, the section below offers a brief preamble to this analysis by outlining key theoretical points about its nature and scope.

Nature and Scope of Key Analysis Underlying the New TEF Metric

In order to prompt understandings of excellent teaching that include internationalisation, realised through social changes that lead to intellectual reciprocity between home and international students, the analysis of UKES items in the TEF needs to be of a nature that will prompt actions at universities that cannot simply be achieved by changing the content of their curricula. Changing the curriculum to be more inclusive of international perspectives is of course important but it is not sufficient when options for inter-cultural learning are negatively impacted by national contexts which form 'the background against which institutions formulate policy and academic staff do or do not engage in internationalisation of the curriculum' (Leask and Bridge 2013, p. 89). That is why this book continually highlights that we need to change the system through introducing metrics that could facilitate the internationalisation outcomes described above. These metrics should be based on 'inviting and accommodating new rationales, alternative paradigms and interpretations [of international students]' (Leask and Bridge 2013, p. 97). They would then capture reciprocity that is observable in the classroom community and that is felt beyond course content, to the extent that when classroom communities have matured enough to think that inclusion of international students as 'equals' is simply *normal*. Normalisation of the view of international students as epistemic equals should therefore be so strong that it will become most obvious when it is absent.

Such was the intended impact of inclusion of international students through processes of internationalisation at home when it was proposed by Crowther and colleagues (2000) in their position paper published by the European Association for International Education (EAIE). In Crowther et al.'s view, internationalisation, conceptualised as changes at home institutions with regards to the curriculum, interactions between home and international students and staff, as well as cultivation of internationally-focused outlook on research and teaching, should be intended to create opportunities for intercultural learning experiences, especially for those home students who are not internationally mobile. Crowther et al. (2000) however cautioned against the counterindicating effects of national policies that prevent efforts at universities to invite greater input from international students today and from turning classrooms into fora for sharing cultural knowledge on equal terms. Internationalisation was meant to be the process of improvement of higher education, through epistemic inclusion of international learners and encouragement of respectful interaction with them (Dunne 2011), making explicit equal approaches to 'other'. National policies and hostile environments can however set constraints which emanate from legislative and regulatory frameworks (those in relation to the UK have been described in Chapter 2) because 'while internationalisation at home is a matter taking place inside higher education institutions, these institutions do not live in a vacuum and are therefore determined in their work by influences and limits set by external actors' (Crowther et al. 2000, p. 2). What is more, if equal approaches to other are not officially assessed through any institutional evaluations, not least in the sense of national league tables or even international university rankings, they are unlikely to be pursued.

The TEF is thus an opportunity to start anew but the exercises needs to rely less on hard-outcomes, or outcomes that already exist and are independent of the teaching process (as shown in Chapter 5, many of the presently measured outcomes can be achieved without any pedagogical input). Instead, the TEF needs to focus more on assessing how these outcomes change with a change in teaching practice. The vice chancellor of Aston University, Dame Julia King, for instance, has already argued for such a change in the TEF and said that the exercise 'must be an evidenced reflection of the impact the university experience has on students, examining how a university supports students to push their academic limits (…) not just how well already successful students maintain their success' (King's opinion piece, cited in *Times Higher Education*, 2015). The present book also argues that the support that is assessed through the TEF has to extend beyond academic learning and should take account of the relevance and benefits of interculturality for students' wider development—in the sense that it will show how students as individuals develop ethics and values of respecting 'others' and recognise that responding to the diversity of international students and responding to the diversity of home students are in fact not two different agendas but one (Jones and Killick 2007).

It is also important for the TEF to recognise that responding to these two types of 'diversity' should not be based on strategies that encourage remedial or pastoral provision for international students, as this may re-enforce their representations as 'deficient'. Marginson (2013, p. 9) argues that international students are often placed in remedial courses 'without their consent and scarcely with their participation, they are remade into the objects of an inchoate mix of paternalistic pastoral care [and] well-meaning efforts to culturally connect'. Through this, however, they 'face violations of human security in all domains of public, institutional and private life and cannot access the full range of human rights' (ibid., p. 9). Being considered as an intellectually equal participant of a classroom community is one of these rights, but is also one that is often denied to international students based on their perceived status as learners who are in 'deficit' and whose knowledges are not scientific.

The TEF can however evoke responses to diversity of international and home students as 'one', but only if it measures whether opportunities for students to engage with knowledges across cultural boundaries have been enabled and encouraged in student courses. As indicated earlier, this can include UKES questions that ask about the extent to which students' courses encourage cross-cultural interactions and whether the overall course experience develops in students skills in understanding others. But the nature of the analysis of these questions has to focus on capturing the social complexities surrounding the development of these skills and how students are encouraged to engage in 'knowledge-exchange' relations. In other words, the nature of the analysis underlying the proposed metric should evoke relationalities that surround changes in host communities that are becoming more and more hybrid through their interconnectedness with global people (Rizvi 2009). It should highlight what students learn through exposure to and participation in these relationalities.

The best way to assess such relational outcomes would of course be through experimental designs such as Randomised Controlled Trials (RCTs). RCTs are presently thought to be the most robust methodology that can 'tease' out the contribution of a specific classroom approach to student outcomes (Spybrook et al. 2016). RCTs however could be very difficult to implement as part of the TEF, due to the complexity of the design and operational matters connected with comparability across universities. They could also trigger some ethical questions as evaluating contributions of the teaching process to realisation of international students as equals through RCTs would mean that certain student groups could be disadvantaged as, for the purposes of the experiment, they would have to attend classrooms in which such realisation is not actively encouraged (so called 'control group').

Universities therefore have to work within the constraints of data that are already collected by the sector. Chapter 7 shows ways in which it is possible to capture *the relational nature* between student characteristics, the characteristics of the teaching process, other organisational factors, inclusion of international students as equals and benefits of such inclusion for home students. Chapter 7 shows how this can be done through multilevel regression analyses of student data, as well as measurements that describe work done in the classroom to include international students on more equal terms. The purpose of Chapter 7 is to show, in practice, how the TEF can appropriate national league tables in relation to excellence in teaching that considers internationalisation understood as a process towards epistemic democracy as one of its determinants. Before moving on to Chapter 7 however, the remaining part of this chapter provides a short critique of the analyses of data in the TEF's sister projects—CALOHEE, AHELO and the CLA. This critique is included because it is intended to identify lessons that can be learnt from the current design of the TEF for other countries. It is hoped that the critique below will deepen policy makers' consciousness about the need to include a similar metric on internationalisation in these three projects. The US is one of the biggest recruiters of international students, which is why the fact that the CLA (being their national assessment closest in equivalence to the TEF) does not consider any metrics on internationalisation is rather disappointing. Continental Europe has already for some time been predicted to 'catch-up' with the UK in international students' recruitment (e.g. Minsky 2015), which means that supra-national projects such as CALOHEE or AHELO, which would involve these countries should these projects finally be implemented, could bring about significant developments in terms of democratisation of universities' relationships with international students; if these were adequately assessed through their relevant metrics. Finally, Australia, a country that has maintained high international enrolments for many years and has recently recorded top levels of international students' enrolments (Marginson 2018), has just announced plans for the replica of the TEF. Although their methodology is not specified yet, the initial analysis indicates that the Australian framework will be very similar to the TEF (Ross 2018). For this reason, the Australian plans are also worth critiquing below, to prevent the same internationalisation pitfalls that the designers of the original TEF have created.

TEF's International Sister Projects

The TEF's international sister projects, CALOHEE, AHELO and the CLA were introduced in Chapter 4. Without going into the details of their design again, it is worth noting here that all these projects aim to develop means of assessing ways in which higher education institutions contribute to specific learner outcomes (discipline specific and 'value-added' skills). These ways, on the one hand, are proposed to be 'measured' taking into account unique characteristics of each subject area and differing university contexts around the world, but on the other, also aim to enable assessments that are comparable internationally, regardless of language, culture and the socio-political context of higher education institutions. Such objectives seem to be contradictory in terms, as the differing national and institutional contexts of universities do not seem to offer any potential for comparisons of 'like with like'. This might be why the projects have received a fair amount of criticism, for example, from Phillip Altbach (2015), who, alongside country representatives that participated in the feasibility study of the AHELO project, recommended that this specific project is ended because 'it seems highly unlikely that a common benchmark can be obtained for comparing achievements in a range of quite different countries' (Altbach 2015, p. 2).

Originally though, AHELO, through its 'metrics', was intending to generate worldwide sector data on (a) generic skills that students in all fields should acquire (e.g. critical thinking, analytical reasoning and problem solving), (b) discipline-specific skills (focusing on applications of information learnt in subject disciplines, (c) the 'value-added' of university education (through measurements of contribution of university teaching and learning to a change in educational outcomes of students), and (d) the impact of contextual factors related to organisational environment and students' backgrounds on generic and discipline specific skills (Shahjahan 2013). The current plans for CALOHEE propose to generate similar data through assessments of student outcomes related to generic and discipline specific knowledge and skills, as well as wider competencies in the field of civic, social and cultural engagement (CALOHEE Policy Note 2017). Finally, the CLA was also set up to test students' critical thinking, analytic reasoning, problem solving, and written communications competencies (Klein et al. 2007). All of these projects emphasise the type of assessments that can show how any of the competencies they test are influenced by the interplay between the education the students receive and the individual characteristics that they bring with them to higher education. This is referred to in the projects as the 'value-added', which, as shown in Chapter 5, is also said to be assessed in the TEF. The problem is that the proposed nature and scope of analyses of data under either of these projects are not capable of capturing this influence.

The previous sections of this chapter have critiqued the validity of 'splitting' the key NSS metrics in the TEF into categories based on students' ethnicity and domicile. It has been argued that these 'splits' do not actually provide any estimates of 'value added', as they do not assess relationships and associations between satisfaction with the course, engagement in the classroom and the teaching process. The methodologies underlying AHELO, CALOHEE and the CLA do not provide any such information either. The three projects propose testing formats that will (or currently) include responding to and analysing footage from real-life situations, applying computer simulation and testing decision making of students through 'work-sample' performance tasks which, while to some extent can be seen to be providing real-time assessments of reasoning and problem-solving skills, at the same do not give any information about the contribution of teaching in students' disciplines to these skills. The focus in CALOHEE, AHELO and the CLA on assessing 'institutional contributions', mostly to academic skills, also draws attention to the fact that, similarly to the TEF, understandings of excellence in teaching is limited to mainly supporting education performance outcomes. The only assessment exercise where excellence in teaching may be seen to also be considering wider social development is CALOHEE, which specifically mentions developing competencies that prepare students for their role in society (CALOHEE Working Paper 2017). The plans for CALOHEE in terms of 'measuring' how well universities prepare students for their role as good citizens may thus offer some potential for also including international students as epistemic equals, as the exercise sets out to test the 'value added' of intuitions in terms of character development of students, leading to more inclusive and equitable civic and social engagement (CALOHEE Working Paper 2017). But as explained in Chapter 4, the proposed methodology to assess these outcomes does not actually focus on the teaching contribution to these outcomes but instead proposes to assess whether students have a certain set of skills or not. It is however important to note that respectful and equitable engagement with international students is explicitly mentioned under CALOHEE as some of the EU countries that will be taking part in CALOHEE may only just be 'getting used to' the changes in society caused by the presence of international students, due to the recent expansion of 'internationalisation' in non-Anglophone countries. Due to the recent political events such as Brexit, decreasing 'attractiveness' of US institutions after the election of Donald Trump and higher education developments in East Asia, which are changing the traditional patterns of international students' mobility (The British Council 2018), many of the EU countries are predicted to be receiving increased numbers of international students for the first time. They therefore may need to be reminded more explicitly that international students deserve civic and 'equitable' engagement.

The assessment of the 'value added' in the CLA is carried out at the level of institution whereby whole schools and programmes are taken as the unit of analysis. The purpose behind the 'whole school' measures is to send a signal to administrators, faculty, and students about some of the additional competencies students in specific faculties can develop, and whether the level of these competencies is better, worse, or about the same as what would be expected, given the ability level of their incoming students. The faculty-and discipline-based assessments are similar to the plans for the subject-level TEF, but equally, just as he TEF does not capture the contribution of teaching to specific developmental outcomes, the CLA methodologies, based on tracking progress of students on real-life tasks and writing argumentative essays, do not show how much of this progress can be explained by specific characteristics of the teaching process on student courses.

Another one of US national assessments, the National Survey of Student Engagement (NSSE) survey, could, on the other hand, go some way in 'measuring' the learning gain through 'value-added', but only if its items (many of which were used to design UKES) were analysed through lenses of relationality. The NSSE survey was launched in 2000 and updated in 2013 to assess the extent to which students engage in educational practices associated with high levels of learning and development. The questionnaire collects information in key categories of participation in specific academic activities (such as, for example, reading or re-drafting work), opinions about challenges of coursework and perceptions of the college environment. The NSSE also aims to estimate students' personal growth since starting college, through questions, for instance, about the frequency of diverse perspectives (in political, religious and ethnic terms), being included in course discussions and assignments. Other NSSE questions also ask the students to reflect on opportunities in their courses to express their own views on the topic, and to examine their strengths and weaknesses by drawing on perspectives of 'others' and imagining what an issue may look like from somebody else's point of view. Such questions at least begin to shape views in the students that it is possible (and desirable) to position 'others' as experts and that their presence is in fact a necessary condition for wider learning gain that students develop through higher education. The next step should therefore be for these perspectives to be measured in national assessment exercises, but not through aggregating scores on the items that ask about engagement with diverse students, as these will still tell us nothing about the role teaching plays in shaping views of international students as epistemic 'equals', but rather through analyses that capture the social complexity of this engagement and the extent to which it is engineered by university tutors.

As such, the latest Australian plans to implement a replicated version of the TEF are quite worrying. The Australian government has recently said that their version of the TEF will introduce measures of student retention, satisfaction, graduate employment and widening access and tie university performance on these measures to the funding institutions will receive. As a result, a new framework for university performance has been proposed by the Regional Universities Network in Australia and it has been agreed that 'providers should be judged on six "core" measures and up to four optional ones, in a system similar to the UK's teaching excellence framework' (Ross 2018, p. 11). The core measures are proposed to be institutional completion and attrition rates, student and employer satisfaction, employment outcomes and share of students from disadvantaged backgrounds. The optional measures include plans to rate universities on graduate starting salaries and student support resources (ibid.). It is no surprise that such plans have spurred a wave of criticism from senior academics who are worried about the new framework rewarding the wrong things (Ross 2018). In the context of this book, what is worrying is the lack of proposals to evaluate how universities realise international students as epistemic equals; these are the same worries that have been deconstructed in Chapter 5 in relation to the TEF. Australia is now predicted to overtake the UK in recruitment of international students (Marginson 2018). Yet, there is nothing in the proposed plans that gives at least the slightest indication that assessments of teaching in the Australian context may include ways in which universities contribute to the epistemic life of international and home students. This could be done in Australia quite easily, seeing that they have already run the Australasian Survey of Student Engagement (AUSSE), which, just as the UKES, has been modelled on the original NSSE developed in the US.

In closing this chapter, it is also important to note that analyses based on surveys such as the NSSE or UKES, as opposed to performance tasks that underlie the CLA, AHELO or most of the CALOHEE indicators, may also be less problematic in terms of comparability of data. From the start, a number of questions about the validity in comparing assessments generated by either AHELO, CALOHEE or even CLA can be raised, as finding a common denominator for comparing 'performance' on a range of real-life tasks can be very difficult. What about the fact that, for example, under the current methodology, each time students could be asked different questions, depending on the specific context of the tasks they would need to perform? These questions could not be asked across many universities in the same way either, as they could not be valid in all contexts for the simple reason that not all universities may teach the same aspects of a chosen discipline. In higher education, courses and curricula vary significantly and it would be hard to image (and unfair to expect) much commonality. Additionally, universities with selective admissions procedures would arguably do better than lower-tariff institutions. The generic skills of critical thinking and communication proposed to be tested under AHELO, CLA and CALOHEE may also be associated with different interpretations of their meanings in different national and institutional contexts. For example, criticality may be understood differently in China than it is in the UK. Furthermore, the difference in understandings of these skills will also vary across disciplines. For instance, students on a business course in one university will want to acquire different communication skills than social science students in another.

But there should be no doubt that criticality and communication skills that lead to respect for students from diverse backgrounds should be understood in the same way everywhere. There is only one understanding that underlies these skills—that of realisation of international students as epistemic equals. And while it would be difficult to test this understanding in 'real-life job' scenarios that currently underlie AHELO, CALOHEE or the CLA, it is much more realistic to ask about them in student engagement surveys. If students are asked in such surveys about engagement with identities and views of others, alongside opportunities for developing own knowledges and ethics, as well as how much they think the teaching on their courses contributes to their engagement with 'others', it is then clear what will be learnt from the results of such surveys. It has however been indicated above that aggregating mean responses under such questions would not be enough, as this would not capture the *relationality* between inclusion and pedagogy. This relationality can only be captured by the type of analyses that are explained in Chapter 7.

References

Altbach, P. G. (2015). AHELO: The myth of measurement and comparability. *International Higher Education, 82,* 2–3.

CALOHEE Policy Note. (2017). *Towards a more reliable model for evidence based learning and quality assurance and enhancement.* Tuning Calohee. Accessed on 26 July 2018. Retrieved from https://www.calohee.eu/wp-content/uploads/2017/11/CALOHEE-Policy-Note.pdf.

CALOHEE Working Paper. (2017). *Calohee working paper for civic, social and cultural engagement.* Tuning Calohee. Accessed on 26 July 2018. Retrieved from https://www.calohee.eu/wp-content/uploads/2016/06/Working-Paper-for-Civic-Social-and-Cultural-Engagement.pdf.

Crowther, P., Joris, M., Otten, M., Nilsson, B., Teekens, H., & Wächter, B. (2000). *Internationalisation at home: A position paper.* Accessed on 26 July 2018. Retrieved from http://citeseerx.ist.psu.edu/viewdoc/summary.

Dunne, C. (2011). Developing an intercultural curriculum within the context of the internationalisation of higher education: Terminology, typologies and power. *Higher Education Research & Development, 30*(5), 609–622.

Grove, J. (2015). NSS results unrelated to teaching quality, study claims. *Times Higher Education.* Accessed on 26 July 2018. Retrieved from https://www.timeshighereducation.com/news/nss-results-unrelated-teaching-quality-study-claims.

Havergal, C. (2015). UK Engagement Survey: Universities have limited impact on students' 'soft' skill development. *Times Higher Education.* Accessed on 26 July 2018. Retrieved from https://www.timeshighereducation.com/news/uk-engagement-survey-universities-have-limited-impact-students-soft-skill-development.

Hayes, A. (2017). The teaching excellence framework in the United Kingdom: An opportunity to include international students as "equals"? *Journal of Studies in International Education, 21*(5), 483–497.

Hayes, A. (2018). Nation boundedness and international students' marginalisation: What's emotion got to do with it? *International Studies in Sociology of Education, 27*(2–3), 288–306.

Jones, E., & Killick, D. (2007). Internationalisation of the curriculum. In E. Jones & S. Brown (Eds.), *Internationalising higher education* (pp. 109–119). London: Routledge.

Jones, S., Pampaka, M., Swain, D., & Skyrme, J. (2017). Contextualising degree-level achievement: An exploration of interactions between gender, ethnicity, socio-economic status and school type at one large UK university. *Research in Post-compulsory Education, 22*(4), 455–476.

King, J. (2015). TEF must become 'evidenced reflection' of the impact of teaching (Dame Julia King's opinion piece published in *Times Higher Education* on 24 July 2015). Accessed on 26 July 2018. Retrieved from https://www.timeshighereducation.com/blog/tef-must-become-evidenced-reflection-impact-teaching.

Klein, S., Benjamin, R., Shavelson, R., & Bolus, R. (2007). The collegiate learning assessment: Facts and fantasies. *Evaluation Review, 31*(5), 415–439.

Leask, B., & Bridge, C. (2013). Comparing internationalisation of the curriculum in action across disciplines: Theoretical and practical perspectives. *Compare: A Journal of Comparative and International Education, 43*(1), 79–101.

Lee, J. J., & Rice, C. (2007). Welcome to America? International student perceptions of discrimination. *Higher Education, 53*(3), 381–409.

Liu, W., & Lin, X. (2016). Meeting the needs of Chinese international students: Is there anything we can learn from their home system? *Journal of Studies in International Education, 20*(4), 357–370.

Malcolm, Z. T., & Mendoza, P. (2014). Afro-Caribbean international students' ethnic identity development: Fluidity, intersectionality, agency, and performativity. *Journal of College Student Development, 55*(6), 595–614.

Marginson, S. (2012). Including the other: Regulation of the human rights of mobile students in a nation-bound world. *Higher Education, 63,* 497–512.

Marginson, S. (2013). Equals or others? Mobile students in a nationally bordered world. In S. Sovic & M. Blythman (Eds.), *International students negotiating higher education* (pp. 9–27). London: Routledge.

Marginson, S. (2018). *The UK in the global student market: Second place for how much longer?* London: Centre for Global Higher Education, UCL Institute of Education.

Minsky, C. (2015). Universities in mainland Europe go head-to-head with the UK. *Times Higher Education.* Accessed on 26 July 2018. Retrieved from https://www.timeshighereducation.com/student/news/universities-mainland-europe-go-head-head-uk.

Mwale, S., Alhawsawi, S., Sayed, Y., & Rind, I. A. (2018). Being a mobile international postgraduate research student with family in the United Kingdom: Conflict, contestation and contradictions. *Journal of Further & Higher Education, 42*(3), 301–312.

Oikonomidoy, E., & Williams, G. (2013). Enriched or latent cosmopolitanism? Identity negotiations of female international students from Japan in the US. *Discourse: Studies in the Cultural Politics of Education, 34*(3), 380–393.

Rizvi, F. (2009). Towards cosmopolitan learning. *Discourse: Studies in the Cultural Politics of Education, 30,* 253–268.

Ross, J. (2018). Australian universities design their own performance funding test. *Times Higher Education.* Accessed on 26 July 2018. Retrieved from https://www.timeshighereducation.com/news/australian-universities-design-their-own-performance-funding-test.

Seeber, M., Cattaneo, M., Huisman, J., & Paleari, S. (2016). Why do higher education institutions internationalize? An investigation of the multilevel determinants of internationalization rationales. *Higher Education, 72*(5), 685–702.

Shahjahan, R. A. (2013). Coloniality and a global testing regime in higher education: Unpacking the OECD's AHELO initiative. *Journal of Education Policy, 28*(5), 676–694.

Spiro, J. (2014). Learning interconnectedness: Internationalisation through engagement with one another. *Higher Education Quarterly, 68,* 65–84.

Spybrook, J., Shi, R., & Kelcey, B. (2016). Progress in the past decade: An examination of the precision of cluster randomized trials funded by the US Institute of Education Sciences. *International Journal of Research & Method in Education, 39*(3), 255–267.

The British Council. (2018, January). *International student mobility to 2027: Local investment, global outcomes.* Education Intelligence Feature, The British Council. Available from https://ei.britishcouncil.org/education-intelligence/ei-feature-international-student-mobility-2027-local-investment-global-outcome.

Toogood, A. (2015, September 15–17). *The expectation-experience gap of higher education tourists.* Paper presented at the annual BERA conference, Belfast.

Tran, L. T. (2016). Mobility as 'becoming': A Bourdieuian analysis of the factors shaping international student mobility. *British Journal of Sociology of Education, 37*(8), 1268–1289.

7

Case Study

This final chapter of the book models UKES data from a case study university to illustrate the theoretical points about the type of data and analysis required for the new metric that were discussed in Chapter 6. The chapter proposes a statistical model for a TEF metric, demonstrating in practice ways in which the TEF can measure internationalisation understood as social change leading to accepting 'others' as equal. The closing section of the chapter discusses domestic and international implications of the new TEF outcomes. It focuses on the moral and professional value of the proposed TEF metric, highlighting opportunities for epistemic inclusion of international students and liberation of home students from the negative policy discourses that prevent them from developing more critical relationships with their international peers. Through multilevel modelling of UKES data, the chapter shows, in practice, ways in which re-structuring of the TEF metrics is possible within the constraints of the sector data that are currently available. The modelling presents the type of analysis that could be used in the TEF to capture levels of intercultural interactions by discipline (based on single subject ratings) at individual universities. It is important to note that the aim of the data modelling presented in this chapter is not to create a 'perfect' metric, but rather to conceptualise its design and analysis, as

© The Author(s) 2019   **155**
A. Hayes, *Inclusion, Epistemic Democracy and International Students*,
https://doi.org/10.1007/978-3-030-11401-5_7

well as to show how it could work in practice, using a sample dataset. UKES data used here could therefore be easily replaced with any other relevant national dataset which can be used to capture issues of intellectual reciprocity and ways in which this reciprocity is engineered by the teaching process. As already noted in this book, UKES data does not actually adequately capture these issues, but is the only dataset currently available in the UK that could be used as an example.

There are many rationales for including a metric capturing the relationship between inter-cultural interactions and teaching in the TEF. The book has highlighted them consecutively in each chapter, but it is worth summarising them again here for better understanding of each of the stages of the analysis presented below.

Firstly, and mainly technically speaking, some of the rationales that should drive the development of such a metric are related to domestic agendas. In March 2018, Sam Gyimah, the Minister of State for Universities, Science, Research and Innovation, launched a consultation on the methodology of the discipline-level TEF. The consultation sought feedback on the proposed design of the TEF at subject-level, specifically on questions about the best approach to subject-level TEF and whether there should be any 'supplementary' metrics that are not captured by the current evaluation criteria. This chapter responds to some of the questions posed in the consultation, highlighting how the proposed metric could bring improvements to the TEF methodology.

The main contribution of the proposed model is however conceptual. The book has argued that the new metric (through its influence as a 'discursive practice' functioning as a commercial ranking) can help the exercise to respond to the diversity agenda in higher education and the growing need to acknowledge international students as 'equals'. Through this, the proposed metric can also re-conceptualise articulations of internationalisation from a strategy that enhances rankings performance to a process that leads to epistemic democracy as, by 'officially' re-positioning international students from economic objects to epistemic 'equals' and qualified 'experts', the TEF can socialise individuals and the whole institutions into thinking about them in such terms. Internationalisation could thus be re-articulated to mean new social and educational interdependencies with international people who should no longer be viewed as bringing a tension between universities' long connection to the nation state and cosmopolitanism, but rather as people who should have an equal say in producing university knowledge. And whilst there are obvious benefits of such reconceptualisations of internationalisation to international students, it is not often considered how getting rid of public policy representations of international students as people who bring tensions to universities could also benefit home students. But it would, because, as the data modelled in Table 7.3 show, when epistemic inclusion of international students is not practised, benefits of internationalisation are not made available to home students, making their education socially unjust, as they feel excluded from the classroom community. The book therefore argues that the proposed TEF metric can liberate home students from the effects of coloniality—that is, a process which, under the influence of public discourses about international students, has operated for a very long time on the basis of cultural, social and political domination over foreign students in an education system (Stein and Andreotti 2017). It is argued here that by allowing this to happen, home students have been denied access to civic and epistemic development arising from internationalisation.

It is argued here that a change in TEF metrics could be a solution to this situation. Arguably, if international and home students have been denied access to just and equitable education by policy representations, in order to change this, there has to be a counter-change in policy that will cancel out such effects. It has been highlighted several times throughout the book that the problem with subordination of international students is mostly systemic, which is why we need to change the system. The rule of logic suggests that we need to fight fire with fire because the best way of defeating the enemy is through the use of their own weapons. It has been argued in the book that in order to change the socially and historically entrenched attitudes towards international students, which have created conditions for their exclusion in the education system, the change has to be systemic because currently, individual efforts to culturally connect have no backing from the political power. Through public policies that continually challenge the intellectual value of international students, university tutors, governors and home students have been socialised into the type of power relations with international students which do not challenge the outdated 'learning order' which supports the idea that nation state perspectives are normative. Thus, the intention of arguments in this book, which propose that we need an official frame to obligate universities to break this learning order, is not to challenge the efforts of those who already try to do it. Rather, the intention here is to deepen readers' consciousness that this order cannot be changed individually when public policies, including the TEF, make universities colonised in mind and practice. Thus, a TEF metric which can help shape a policy discourse that affords knowledge production to *all* people is proposed below. As such, the proposed metric has the potential to change the philosophy behind learning, not as a process that takes place by acquiring normative contents and structures set by nation states, but one that is rather constitutive of global interconnectedness between diverse forms of political, economic, social, and cultural 'knowledges'. And again, the point of suggesting that this metric is part of the TEF is not to say that individuals do not practise such philosophy already, but rather to turn this practice into a matter of *national importance*.

The Model

The model below offers a design for a TEF metric that measures levels of *relationality* between democratic realisation of international students as epistemic equals in the course community, characteristics of the teaching process that encourage equal and respectful interactions between home and international students, other organisational factors, as well as student individual characteristics. Thus, the outcomes that the proposed TEF metric measures are centered around finding out how a student's (international and home) sense of belonging to their course community change with the characteristics of the teaching process.

The UK Engagement Survey (UKES) data were chosen to design the proposed metric because UKES is already distributed across the sector and can be used for comparisons across universities. The wide use of UKES across the UK also reduces the proportionality of cost of participation for providers and the cost of delivery for the government. It is of course recommended that if UKES were to become a part of the TEF metrics, it would have to be made compulsory for those universities who want to take part in the exercise.

UKES is presently the only national survey that asks about engagement with students and reciprocal relationships students and staff develop in the classroom. The questions in the UKES survey also ask about the degree to which the students think certain relationships or attitudes towards diverse students have been encouraged by their overall course experience. Thus, for the model, UKES questions that are the closest in providing information about whether students feel they have been democratically included as equally qualified knowers in their course community and whether they have been explicitly encouraged by their courses to be part of this community were chosen. Items that ask students to indicate whether the overall course experience contributed to developing their understanding of people from diverse backgrounds, and whether alongside developing these understandings, the students had opportunities to develop and clarify their personal views and ethics were also considered. It has been argued throughout this book that such reciprocity should underlie interactions in democratic classrooms, leading to inclusion of international students as equals, not through overemphasising their identities, because, for instance, universities may try to repair the damage caused by the hostile immigration environment, but rather through inviting in the classroom explorations of complimentary effects of both types of identities and knowledges of people, and how these effects engage both groups of students as 'equals'. It is shown below how the TEF metric based on the selected UKES data can appropriate such understandings.

The analysis of responses to UKES for each course was of course adjusted for student individual characteristics to see how much student-related factors (see Table 7.1 'student predictors') and/or 'course' factors (see Table 7.1 'course predictors') contributed to students' sense of belonging to their classroom communities. Despite stating in the opening statement of the questionnaire that UKES is a survey that is about how students' have been supported to engage with their *'courses'* and that *'course'* is used in the questionnaire to refer to students' *programme of study*, the survey left a number of critics wondering whether some of

160   A. Hayes

Table 7.1 UKES questions proposed to be part of the design of the TEF metric on internationalisation and student predictors

TEF outcome (dependent variable)	Course predictors (independent) variables—related to the teaching on the course
Thinking of your current view of the course as a whole, to what extent do you agree or disagree that… a. I feel part of a community of staff and students 1. Definitely agree 2. Mostly agree 3. Neither agree nor disagree 4. Mostly disagree 5. Definitely disagree	Question a During the current academic year, how much have you been encouraged to do the following activities? a. Contributing to a joint community of staff and students (very much, quite a bit, some, very little) Question b How much has your overall student experience contributed to your knowledge, skills and personal development in the following areas? b. Developing or clarifying personal values or ethics (very much, quite a bit, some, very little) Question c How much has your overall student experience contributed to your knowledge, skills and personal development in the following areas? c. Understanding people of other backgrounds (economic, racial/ethnic, political, religious, nationality, etc.) (very much, quite a bit, some, very little) Student Predictors (independent variables) related to student characteristics 1. UK vs. non-UK 2. Course studied

its items ask about experiences in the classroom or more broadly, about experiences of the university. It is possible to see how questions such as 'During the current academic year, how much have you been encouraged to do the following activities?', with the answer being 'Contributing to a joint community of staff and students' can suggest that it might also be about engagement beyond the classroom, which is why it is recommended that questions that may create such ambiguity may be re-written, should the proposed metric be implemented under the TEF, to include more specific references to 'classroom/course community'. Phrases such as 'During the current academic year …' should also be replaced with 'During your current course …' or 'Has the teaching on your current

7 Case Study 161

course ...?'. As indicted at the start of the chapter, the design for the proposed metric was conceptualised working within the constraints of the data that are currently collected by the sector. So, the aim here was to theorise the design and analysis of a metric that could support key points in this book—namely, that *it is* possible to create a metric that provides information about relationalities between the characteristics of the teaching process, inclusion and epistemic democracy. The point of this chapter and the modelling of UKES data presented below is to show how such a metric could work in practice, rather than to design a 'perfect metric'.

In the proposed metric, the specific outcomes that are measured are related to the *experience of the course* (see 'Dependent Variable' in Table 7.1), in relation to questions a–c and taking account of student characteristics listed in Table 7.1.

Due to the ordinal nature of student responses to the UKES survey and because students who normally participate in UKES are clustered within subjects, a multilevel regression model that takes into account the ordinal nature of the responses and the hierarchical structure of UKES data (i.e. ratings of individual students that are nested in courses) was used in the analysis. In addition, it was also recognised that there might be some 'contextual' factors operating at individual course level, which may be contributing to differences in student responses between courses. That is why the regression model that was used included 'random effects' that were measured at course level.

The following random intercept cumulative model for ordinal data was used in the analysis, using the R package.

$$logit\left(\gamma_{cij}\right) = \alpha_c - (x_{ij}'\boldsymbol{\beta} + \mu_j)$$

where $j = 1, 2, \ldots.n$ is the course index and

i is the student index

γ_{cij}: the cumulative probability for student i on course j on the dependent variable.

α_c: the mean effect on the cumulative probability up to c-th category (c are categories of responses on an ordinal scale, including 1—Definitely agree, 2—Mostly agree, 3—Neither agree nor disagree, 4—Mostly disagree, 5—Definitely disagree).

162   A. Hayes

$x'_{ij}\beta$: the effect (on the cumulative probability) caused by course predictors (independent variables).

μ_j: the random effect (on the cumulative probability) caused by different courses.

The cumulative model uses cumulative probabilities up to a threshold, therefore making the range of student responses binary at the threshold. The answer 'some' in each of the predictor variables at the course level was the threshold in this analysis (i.e. cut off point—coded in Fig. 7.1. below as 0), meaning that students' answers above 'some' were considered to be a positive response (i.e. 'very much' and 'quite a bit') and answers below 'some'—as a negative response (i.e. 'very little'). The specific codes and 'labelling' of variables that was used in the R package are presented in Fig. 7.1.

Due to the coding of data explained in Fig. 7.1, the results in Tables 7.2 and 7.3 corresponding to each predictor variable at the course level—that is, 'contribution' (referring to question "a" in course predictors in Table 7.1), 'development' (referring to question "b" in course predictors in Table 7.1) and 'understanding' (referring to question "c" in Table 7.1), represent probabilities for students who answered 'very little'. This also means that the baseline student in Tables 7.2 and 7.3 (labelled as 'baseline') was a student who responded 'some' to 'contribution', 'development' and 'understanding' 'questions'. Estimations for a baseline student were run first (with no predictor variables) for

Independent Variable	Labels
Question a	Contribution
Question b	Development
Question c	Understanding
Answers to each of the independent variable	Coding used to create threshold levels
Very much	-2
Quite a bit	-1
Some	0
Very little	1

Fig. 7.1 Coding and labels for independent variables used in R

Table 7.2 Estimates, standard errors, p-values (in parentheses) and predicted probabilities of feeling part of community

International students—Subject Group A						
Threshold	Estimates	Std. Error	Definitely agree	Mostly agree	Neither agree nor disagree	Definitely disagree
First	−7.2543	2.2405				
Second	−1.1790	1.1891				
Third	4.673	0.7128				
Baseline			**0.0007**	**0.2345**	**0.7495**	**0.0153**
Slopes (for students answering 'very little')						
Contribution	2.1978	0.7501 (0.0034)	7.851×10^{-5}	0.0330	0.84455	0.1225
Development	−0.2768	0.9034 (0.7593)	0.0009	0.2877	0.6998	0.1161
Understanding	2.6672	0.9684 (0.0059)	4.91×10^{-5}	0.0209	0.7967	0.1824
Random Effects						
Course level						
σ_μ	3.849×10^{-5}					
ICC	4.5035×10^{-10}					

Table 7.3 Estimates, standard errors, p values (in parentheses) and predicted probabilities of feeing part of the community

Home students—Subject Group B							
Threshold	Estimates	Std. Error	Definitely agree	Mostly agree	Neither agree nor disagree	Mostly disagree	Definitely disagree
First	−1.9791	0.5328					
Second	−0.1035	0.4809					
Third	1.6781	0.5402					
Fourth	2.3495	0.5969					
Baseline			**0.1214**	**0.3527**	**0.3685**	**0.0702**	**0.0871**
Slopes (for students answering 'very little')							
Contribution	0.9664	0.2960 (0.0011)	0.0499	0.2055	0.4154	0.1287	0.2005
Development	0.7151	0.3723 (0.0548)	0.0633	0.2427	0.4177	0.1130	0.1632
Understanding	0.0227	0.3484 (0.9480)	0.1190	0.3495	0.3711	0.0715	0.0889
Random Effects							
Course level							
σ_μ	0.5191						
ICC	0.0757						

purposes of comparison with estimations that were run later including course effects. This comparison helped to illustrate how the variability in student answers changed, when different course characteristics were considered.

Table 7.2 presents results for international students studying 'Subject Group A' courses and Table 7.3 presents results for home students studying courses in 'Subject Group B'. The two labels 'Subject Group A' and 'Subject Group B' were used to preserve the anonymity of data that were used in the analysis. Data from only one faculty are included below (from 366 students, clustered under 17 courses). The model can of course be used with larger samples from many faculties across any university (it is generally expected that in statistical models like this one, larger samples would give more robust results) but it was important to check here whether the model would also work with smaller samples (i.e. whether the model would work with courses that do not have many students). Separate analyses for each course were run, for home and international students, which were then grouped under subject-disciplines, using Level 2 of the Common Aggregation Hierarchy system (CAH2) developed by the Higher Education Statistics Agency (HESA) in the UK to group higher education subjects. CAH2 is proposed to be used in subject-level TEF. CAH2 divides courses into 7 subject groups, including: medical and health sciences, engineering and technology, natural sciences, social sciences, business and law, arts, and humanities. The results below are from two of these groups, which, for anonymity, were coded 'Subject Group A' and 'Subject Group B'.

Results and Interpretation

The results in Table 7.2 show that the characteristics of teaching on courses in 'Subject Group A' have an overall effect on international students sense of the course community. The results indicate that the teaching on these courses characterised by the lack of reciprocity and intercultural relationships is associated negatively with international students' sense of belonging as 'equal'. This can be seen, for example, in responses in the column 'definitely disagree', whereby the baseline probability of 0.0153 for students who do not feel part of the community of staff and students (i.e. those answering 'definitely disagree') changes to 0.1225 for students whose course did not encourage them to make contributions to this community and to 0.1824 for students who presumably were not encouraged to engage with the cultures and identities of home students because they indicated that their course experience did not develop in them understanding of people from other racial/ethnic, political and economic backgrounds. By extension, the baseline probability of 0.2345 of students who generally felt they were part of the community decreased to 0.0209 for students who indicated that their courses did not develop in them skills of understanding people from other backgrounds, showing negative effects of the characteristics of the teaching process on their sense of belonging. The small number for random effects (3.849×10^{-5}) indicates that there were no unobserved effects in student ratings at course level within 'Subject Group A' courses and even smaller number for ICC (4.5035×10^{-10}) shows that the results in Table 7.2 cannot be explained by unobserved 'contextual' differences on these courses. ICC is an inferential statistic that can be used when quantitative measurements are made on units that are organized into groups (as is the case of units in this sample analysis). It describes how strongly units in the same group resemble each other. Thus, the small numbers for both, σ_{μ} and ICC suggest that the effects of all predictor variables were more or less the same across all courses in 'Subject Group A'.

Seeing that the covariate 'development' is insignificant (0.7593), another model with only two covariates of 'contribution' and 'understanding' was also tried. The results generated in the second model were nearly identical to the parameters provided in Table 7.2. This means that this covariate does not affect the predictions in the table. No 'random effects' also means that in this particular case, a model without random effects would be a better fit, but for clarification purposes, random effects were included to illustrate how the results should be interpreted. There is no column 'mostly disagree' in Table 7.2 because no students in this sample chose this answer.

Results for home students in 'Subject Group B' are presented in Table 7.3. As highlighted throughout this book, estimations of the extent to which home students' belonging to a community of staff and students may be affected by teaching processes that encourage them to work with students from other backgrounds are important for the conclusions about the broader benefits of internationalisation. The results from the students in 'Subject Group B' show that there are some random effects of contextual factors of courses within this group (0.5191), suggesting that the effects of the teaching process are slightly different for each course in that group of subjects. The ICC figure in the table (0.0757) shows that 7.5% of the total variability of the results (probabilities for students feeling part of the classroom community) can be explained by unobserved (contextual) heterogeneity at course level. The overall direction of changes in probabilities is the same as in the case of international students from 'Subject Group A' courses that we presented in Table 7.2, i.e. that the probability of being part of the community decreases for students whose overall experience on the course did not develop in them skills of working with students from other backgrounds and clarifying their own views and ethics (in fact, the estimates for most students in all courses showed a similar direction). The relationships between a decreased sense of belonging as 'equal' and teaching characterised by lack of reciprocity between home and international students can be seen in Table 7.3, for instance, in the 'definitely agree' column, whereby the probability of 0.1214 of baseline students who strongly felt they were part of the community decreased to 0.0633 if their courses did not develop in them skills in clarifying personal values and to 0.1190 if they were not taught to understand students from other backgrounds. Similarly, baseline students who 'mostly disagreed' they were part of the community (0.0702) were even more likely to disagree if they were not encouraged to make a contribution to this community (0.1287), not to develop their own views and ethics (0.1130) and whose courses did not develop in them skills in understanding of 'others' (0.0715).

The observed *relational* nature of predictor variables showing that in subject disciplines where students (both home and international)

168   A. Hayes

are encouraged to be part of the classroom community, and where the overall experience of their courses encourages respect for one another, through complimentary effects of learning about 'others' and creating opportunities for 'others' to learn about 'self', has important implications for the subject-level TEF methodology. These are discussed in the section that follows.

Domestic Implications

The sample analysis presented above was based on the same classification of disciplines as in the Level 2 of the Common Aggregation Hierarchy system (CAH2) (see Fig. 7.2) which, at the time of writing, was proposed to be used in subject-level TEF (DfE 2018). Most categories of courses/disciplines that are captured in the categories included in the UKES survey, to cluster student responses under disciplinary groups, seem to match those that are also included in CAH2 (Fig. 7.3). Information that UKES collects about student disciplines could be easily grouped under the 7 categories and 35 subjects included in CAH2.

Furthermore, the classification of disciplinary and subject data in UKES could also enable capturing interdisciplinary provision, in particular, for joint and multi-subject combined courses. Again, at the time of writing, the subject-level TEF consultation document (DfE 2018) proposed that the two subjects which make up a course are treated in the same way as their equivalent single subject programmes. This could be easily supported by the way the UKES collects data about disciplines as the questionnaire asks students to identify 'core' disciplines in cases where these are part of combined and multi-subject courses.

Finally, the subject-level consultation on the TEF also sought to identify whether there should be more 'supplementary' metrics with regards to areas that are currently not considered in the exercise. The answer to this question is 'yes' and this supplementary metric should focus on assessing internationalisation in the ways that have been identified in this book. The design and theoretical basis for this metric have been conceptualised throughout the book and this chapter in particular has shown how it could work in practice. The core idea underlying

Subject groups	CAH2 Codes	35 CAH2 subjects
Medical and health sciences	CAH010-010 CAH020-010 CAH020-020 CAH040-010 CAH020-090 CAH050-010 CAH030-020	1.Medicine & dentistry 2.Nursing 3.Pharmacology, toxicology and pharmacy 4.Psychology 5.Subjects allied to medicine 6.Veterinary science 7.Sport & exercise sciences
Engineering and technology	CAH110- 010CAH100- 010CAH100-070	8.Computing 9.Engineering 10.Technology
Natural sciences	CAH060-010 CAH030-010 CAH070-020 CAH090-010 CAH070-010 CAH070-030 CAH080-010	11.Agriculture, food and related studies 12.Biosciences 13.Chemistry 14.Mathematical sciences 15.Physics and astronomy 16.Physical, material and forensic sciences 17.General and others in sciences
Social sciences	CAH130-010 CAH150-020 CAH120-010 CAH150-030 CAH150-010 CAH220-010 CAH150-040	18.Architecture, building and planning 19.Economics 20.Geographical and environmental studies 21.Politics 22.Sociology, social policy and anthropology 23.Education and teaching 24.Health and social care
Business and law	CAH170- 010CAH160-010	25.Business and management26.Law
Arts	CAH210-010	27.Creative arts and design
Humanities	CAH190-020 CAH180-010 CAH190-010 CAH190-040 CAH200-010 CAH140-010 CAH200-020 CAH230-010	28.Celticstudies 29.Communications and media studies 30.English studies 31.Languages, linguistics and classics 32.History and archaeology 33.Humanities & liberalarts 34.Philosophy & religious studies 35.Combined and general studies

Fig. 7.2 Proposed subject groups for subject-level TEF based on the Level 2 of the Common Aggregation Hierarchy system—adapted from DfE (2018). Teaching Excellence and Student Outcomes Framework: subject-level: Consultation document, available from https://consult.education.gov.uk/higher-education-reform/teaching-excellence-and-student-outcomes-framework/

this metric is that is has the potential to fight the symptoms of public policies that have led to subordination of international students due to coloniality and to remove the limits on home students' agency to engage with their international peers on socially and politically equal terms. Realising such changes would be the core outcome to be assessed, creating intentions towards working to achieve such changes and an agreed frame that will obligate universities to make them.

170   A. Hayes

> 40. Please indicate which of the following most closely matches your discipline. If you are unsure of which subject your course should be placed in, please click 'More Info'. Please note that a) if you are undertaking teacher training, you should select 'Teacher Training' rather than the discipline you aim to teach; b) if you are studying management or business in relation to a particular discipline then you should select that discipline (e.g. nursing, tourism, computer science):
>
> - Teacher Training (please indicate this if you are undertaking Teacher Training - not the discipline that you teach)
> - Education studies (including Research Skills in Education; and Academic Studies in Education)
> - Social Work (including Child Care and Community Work)
> - Medicine and Dentistry
> - Medical Science and Pharmacy (including Anatomy; Neuroscience; Pharmacology; Physiology and Pathology)
> - Nursing (including Midwifery)
> - Other subjects allied to Medicine (for example: Aural and Oral sciences; Nutrition; Public Health; Medical Technology)
> - Biology and related Sciences (including Biochemistry, Ecology, Genetics, and Microbiology)
> - Sports Science (including Sport Coaching, Sport Development, Sport Studies)
> - Psychology
> - Veterinary Sciences (for example: Pre-Clinical and Clinical Veterinary Medicine)
> - Agriculture and related subjects (for example: Food & Beverage Studies; Animal Science; Environmental Conservation)
> - Physical Science (for example: Physics; Chemistry; Forensic and Archaeological Science; Geology)
> - Physical Geography and Environmental Science
> - Mathematical Sciences (including Statistics and Operations Research)
> - Computer Science
> - Mechanically-based Engineering (including Aerospace Engineering; Production & Manufacturing Engineering)
> - Electronic and Electrical Engineering
> - Civil and Chemical Engineering (and other Engineering not covered above)
> - Technology (for example: Biotechnology; Maritime Technology; and Materials Technology)
> - Architecture; Building and Planning
> - Human and Social Geography
> - Sociology; Social Policy and Anthropology
> - Politics (including International Studies)
> - Law
> - Economics
> - Business (including Marketing)
> - Management (including Human Resource Management)
> - Finance and Accounting
> - Tourism; Transport; Travel (and others in Business and Administrative studies not covered above)
> - Media studies (including Media Production)
> - Communications and Information studies (including Publishing and Journalism)
> - English-based studies (for example: English Language; English Literature; Scots Literature)
> - European Languages and Area studies
> - Other Languages and Area studies
> - History and Archaeology
> - Philosophy; Theology and Religious studies
> - Art and Design
> - Performing Arts (including Music; Dance; and Drama)
> - Other Creative Arts (for example: Cinematics; Photography; Crafts)
> - Combined

Fig. 7.3 Categories of courses and disciplines asked about in the UKES (Adapted from UKES Questionnaire 2017)

It has been argued earlier in the book that retaining the existing elements based on the 'split' NSS metrics by students' domicile is unlikely to lead to any social developments at universities in terms of accepting globally mobile people as intellectual 'equals'. But if the TEF has a ranking that 'measures' these developments at subject-level, the exercise is likely to focus universities' attention on this aspect of student learning and prompt pedagogies in these subjects that may encourage more meaningful inter-cultural exchanges. It has been shown above how the extent to which these pedagogies are practised can be measured. It is also important to highlight the type of information 'random effects' can provide, as values associated with σ_u and ICC can help explain the levels of variability in these pedagogies in individual subjects and across all disciplinary groups. The regression model that was used in the sample analysis in this chapter included estimates of 'random effects', that were measured at subject level, to be able to assess how much of the predicted probabilities of students' belonging to a course community can be explained by differing commitment to inter-cultural learning across student courses. The proposed model therefore allows for the distribution of ratings to vary naturally between the subjects, which again, at the time of writing, was one of the key questions in the TEF consultation, asking whether it was possible to show such a variation (DfE 2018).

The consultation exercise also asked for proposals with regards to the ways in which the TEF metrics can be more 'meaningful for students' and represent 'value for money' (DfE 2018). As shown in Tables 7.2 and 7.3, the proposed metric can generate information for students about how welcoming and inclusive of international students UK universities are. Market intelligence from QS Solutions (International Students Survey 2018) has shown that international students look at TEF rankings, seeking information about levels of international students' satisfaction within their chosen course, teaching quality and how welcoming universities are. In the context of value for money, it was also found in the survey that teaching quality seems to be a major driver of value for money for international students. Thus, metrics such as those proposed in this chapter, that address questions of reciprocal engagement with international students and democratic conditions for their participation in higher education learning, can provide international students with the information they need.

It is also widely known that home students are increasingly looking for evidence of the value for money they pay for higher education. Relevant literature from the field has shown that, in the context of political debates about whether students should be paying over £ 9000 for their university education, there are persistent questions about what they are *actually* paying for (e.g. Jones 2010; Miller 2010). The latest report from the National Audit Office, for instance, says 'if English universities were banks, they would be investigated for mis-selling, as students say they do not get value for money' (cited in Adams 2017), with earlier reports highlighting that the rationales behind the introduction of fees were mainly driven by institutional and economic self-interests (Greenaway and Haynes 2003). Value for money in the context of university fees has been deconstructed by students in terms of universities not providing enough contact hours, their education not leading to satisfactory employment and not providing opportunities for wider-learning gain as the courses are perceived to be focused mostly on feeding employer requirements (e.g. Morgan 2014). The metrics proposed in this chapter respond particularly strongly to the 'wider learning gain' questions, in the sense of students' civic development through intercultural learning and enabling the students to see the intellectual benefits that arise from internationalisation.

Where to from Here? International Implications

This chapter has established that it is possible, using some sector data, to carry out the types of analyses which make it possible to assess the levels of pedagogical intentionality that aims to include international students as 'equals'. The sections above have outlined how this can be done in the UK example. The analysis that has been conducted can also be easily applied in other international contexts, due to the nature and scope of the proposed metric, how the proposed metric uses the national data, as well as the outcomes that are measured. All these make it possible to work with data in any national context.

Firstly, what is uniquely making the metric applicable in other international contexts is the fact the 'teaching standards' driving the pedagogical intentionality that underlies it are those that mean equal, just and free from coloniality education experience. Achieving these standards means consistently maintaining them where they already exist, and leading to transformations in the classroom culture where they are absent; and then maintaining them afterwards. What is even more important is the fact that these standards are not measured by any external indicators, nor there is a cut off point for them. The transformation that is either started or maintained is therefore not assessed against any external indicators, but what is rather evaluated is whether this transformation is consistently delivered. In that sense, it is not an end in itself, but a means to creating conditions for international and home students democratic participation in higher education learning. There are therefore no 'national' factors that could prevent teaching policies from measuring it or that could create bias or inconsistencies in those measurements, which could in turn prevent comparability between various national contexts.

Pedagogical intentionality as consistency in delivering transformation has no targets for levels of inclusion and epistemic justice, which is why the proposed TEF metric aims to identify whether it is practised or not. That is the outcome that is measured by this metric, not whether it meets any benchmarks. Setting a 'target' standard for inclusion or a 'benchmark' would be daft and invalid, as classrooms around the world are likely to have different 'specifications' (i.e. the composition of students answering engagement surveys, and also populations that are likely to be excluded, will vary in different context). Taking these differences into account, the proposed metric therefore measures the relational nature between student characteristics and the teaching process, which means that the differences in population or subject-disciplines will not affect the overall outcomes measured. Rather the point is to show how each classroom performs according to its own specifications.

The main undercurrent of the proposed metric is that it 'measures' epistemic democracy as a relative concept. There are no absolutes against which this output can be assessed—this makes the metric *apolitical* as the focus on the education process allows for any politics related to internationalisation to be put aside. As such, the metric can be used for international comparisons as the relativity that underlies it removes the need to find a common denominator as a basis for comparison. When used in individual national contexts, the metric would compare universities' commitment to epistemic democracy according to their own specifications (and therefore can be used with any national data, at subject level, and also including more diverse populations that may be experiencing issues of non-democratic treatment—such as indigenous populations or BAME groups). All countries and universities would however be assessing the same core idea—that is, whether socially just, unprejudiced and free from coloniality education is practised. The proposed metric therefore responds to the growing critiques of TEF's sister projects such as the CLA, AHELO or CALOHEE, which, as shown earlier in the previous chapter, leave out more critical 'measurements' of internationalisation as one of the determinants of higher education quality and outcomes.

There are of course some limitations of the proposed model. They are, as already alluded to in the opening section of this chapter, mainly related to the ambiguity of the UKES questions, which should be re-written to make it explicit that they ask about classroom learning and to put more emphasis on epistemic democracy. But, taking these constraints into account and also bearing in mind that UKES is presently the only national survey that asks about engagement, the aim here was not to create a 'perfect' metric, but rather to conceptualise its design and analysis, and to show how it could work in practice. Even with the current limitations of the data, the proposed model supports the key idea of this chapter—namely, that it is possible to create a metric that provides information about *relationalities* between the characteristics of the teaching process and realisation of students as epistemic equals. The original UKES questions can always be updated or, for example, in countries that do not presently have national surveys about engagement, new ones can be created.

Some of the student samples that were used in the modelling of UKES data were small. This does not however mean that the analysis proposed here cannot predict probabilities for small samples of international students; rather, some of the small samples used in the analysis produced insignificant results. But as also shown above, despite having non-reportable metrics on some courses, it is still possible to produce group results (Tables 7.2 and 7.3), which would show if these non-reportable metrics had any effects on the group ratings. The analysis presented in Tables 7.2 and 7.3 considered all three predictor variables ('contribution', 'development' and 'understanding') simultaneously in one regression model. In cases where the model with all three variables presented insignificant results, analyses with only one predictor variable at a time were run. These on the other hand produced significant results. In cases of non-reportable metrics, universities could therefore consider running separate analyses for each predictor variable. However, this could be time consuming and not capture the complexity of inter-cultural relations that are intended to be evoked through combining all three predictor variables in one analysis. Based on the various analyses of models with only one predictor variable, and then subsequent models combining two or three predictors together, for individual courses but also merging them under disciplines using CAH2, it is generally recommended that universities include results from international students if they constitute at least 10% of the whole student population on a given course, or only from those courses that present significant results.

References

Adams, R. (2017). University students failed by rip-off fees, says watchdog. *The Guardian*. Accessed on 31 July 2018. Retrieved from https://www.theguardian.com/education/2017/dec/08/university-students-failed-by-rip-off-fees-says-watchdog.

DfE (Department for Education). (2018). *Teaching Excellence and Student Outcomes Framework: Subject-level Consultation document*. Accessed on 02 Mar 2019. Available from https://consult.education.gov.uk/higher-education-reform/teaching-excellence-and-student-outcomes-framework/supporting_documents/Teaching%20Excellence%20and%20Student%20Outcomes%20Framework%20subjectlevel.pdf.

Greenaway, D., & Haynes, M. (2003). Funding higher education in the UK: The role of fees and loans. *The Economic Journal, 113*(485), 150–166.

International Students Survey. (2018). *QS Enrolment Solutions*. Accessed on 3 Mar 2019. Available from https://www.internationalstudentsurvey.com/international-student-survey-2018/.

Jones, G. (2010). Managing student expectations: The impact of top-up tuition fees. *Perspectives: Policy and Practice in Higher Education, 14*(2), 44–48.

Miller, B. (2010). The price of higher education: How rational is British tuition fee policy? *Journal of Higher Education Policy and Management, 32*(1), 85–95.

Morgan, J. J. (2014). Student experience survey highlights unhappiness over value of money. *Times Higher Education*, (2153), 6–7.

Stein, S., & de Oliveira Andreotti, V. (2017). Higher education and the modern/colonial global imaginary. *Cultural Studies, Critical Methodologies, 17*(3), 173–181.

8

Concluding Remarks

Dehumanisation, which marks not only those whose humanity has been stolen, but also (though in a different way) those who have stolen it, is a distortion of the vocation of becoming more fully human. This distortion occurs within history, but it is not a historical vocation. (…) Dehumanization, although a concrete historical fact, is not a given destiny but the result of an unjust order that engenders violence in the oppressors, which in turn dehumanizes the oppressed (Freire 1970, p. 18)

Internationalisation of higher education should lead to the idea of democratisation of knowledge—that is, in the sense of leading towards institutional epistemic justice (Anderson 2012) whereby universities actively seek epistemic democracy—that is, 'universal participation on terms of equality of all inquirers' (Anderson 2012, p. 172). When epistemic democracy is understood in that sense, it prevents the type of 'dehumanisation' captured by the above quote from Freire (1970). How this happens has been explored in detail in Part II of the book. The simple truth however is that when epistemic democracy is not adopted by institutions, universities 'undermine the epistemic standing of the disadvantaged and block the contribution to inquiry they could have made, had they been able to participate on terms of equality with others'

© The Author(s) 2019
A. Hayes, *Inclusion, Epistemic Democracy and International Students*,
https://doi.org/10.1007/978-3-030-11401-5_8

(Anderson 2012, 171). This is exactly what Dahl (2000), who was cited in the preface to this book, said about factors that prevent the creation of democratic associations—i.e. ones that have been used in the book to illustrate the philosophical basis of the proposed TEF metric.

Democratisation of knowledge production through epistemic equalisation of all knowers has not however been embraced by universities, not least in the UK case where, as shown in Chapter 2, internationalisation's long connection to imperialism and the nation state, as well as its associated policy representations of international students, create a tension with respect to internationally-mobile students as credible inquirers and 'knowers'. Consequently, these students are turned into the oppressed. The imperial connection also makes home students and university tutors colonised in mind and practice and, by the vocation of history, turns them into the oppressors. The details of the type of historical vocation that has had such effects in the UK have also been discussed in Chapter 2. In these concluding remarks, it is however important to recall Freire's (1970) premise that dehumanisation of individuals in the education system is not a given destiny. This premise legitimises conclusions that the dehumanising effects of historical vocation, for both, the oppressed and the oppressor, can be reversed by the TEF metrics this book has outlined. Evidence in Table 7.3, in particular, which shows that home students present higher levels of belonging to a classroom community on courses where everybody is treated as an epistemic equal, provide particular support for this argument. Arguably, the results in Table 7.3 can simultaneously be taken to mean that home students are in fact willing to accept international students as epistemic equals but, influenced for too long by public policy discourses, as well as projects of coloniality that have traditionally encouraged home students to assume positions of superiority, they lack agency to do it. When public policy continually creates unequal conditions for participation of international students in the social and educational life of the country of education, as it has been the case in the UK and elsewhere (Hayes 2018; Marginson 2013; Lee and Rice 2007), students (and university tutors) internalise the idea that such inequality is the truth and 'feel threatened if that truth is questioned' (Freire 1970, 13). What happens as a result is that 'the oppressed are afraid to embrace freedom, and the

8 Concluding Remarks 179

oppressors are afraid of losing the freedom to oppress' (ibid., 20). This leads to situations whereby a 'single path of human progress and of the universal value of Western knowledge' (Stein et al. 2016, p. 4) is pursued, reinforcing home-based knowledge production as superior and international students' constructions as lacking moral and intellectual capacity. But this is where the pursuit of institutional epistemic justice, in the sense of emphasising the epistemic standing of international students and not challenging the contribution to intellectual inquiry they can make is especially important, so institutions can create a different type of 'truth'. This book has argued that this pursuit can be supported by a supplementary TEF metric which, functioning as a policy discourse and a master power, has the potential to socialise people into accepting that alternative knowledges, beyond the home perspectives, can also be the truth. Such metric is then likely to engender actions to practise that alternative truth (Foucault 1969, re-printed in English on 2002).

Freedom from coloniality is acquired by conquest, not by gift, and it is not entirely dependent on histories. That is why freedom must be pursued constantly and responsibly through the type of classroom activism which, as explained in Chapters 3 and 4, does not enable coloniality or encourage pedagogies of reparation or even 'harm-reduction' techniques. This activism should rather be oriented towards equivalence of international students' knowledge and through that, also towards liberating the home student from thinking that this knowledge is not valid. This can happen when learning (and teaching) is forged *with*, and not *for* the oppressed or *by* the oppressor. This in turn means true solidarity, through reciprocal dialogue with international students' intellectual traditions, but without compromising the solidarity owed to home students (hence the UKES items in the proposed metric that encourage understandings of others but also clarifying 'own' views and ethics). It is only when complimentary effects of such exchanges are encouraged, the type of classroom reality that turns people into the oppressed and the oppressors for one another can be transformed.

This book has probably upset some people by suggesting that we need more rankings. But just as we need to reconfigure, for instance, the systems in the financial institutions to prevent poverty, we also need to re-design universities, as institutions responsible for producing knowledge, to prevent epistemic injustice and to stop the damaging effects of coloniality. This simple logic supports the key argument behind creating yet another TEF metric, for the simple reason that when injustices are systemic, they require systemic cures! Systemic cures have to be large scale, just like the rankings, because only when they become like rankings, they will make institutions accountable for how they act collectively. In the current climate of commercialisation of higher education, it is exactly those rankings that create unequal lines of knowledge production. Because of rankings, inequalities are established along the lines of who is perceived to be more useful in the sense of winning institutional rivalry (Hazelkorn 2015; Naidoo 2016). This results in dehumanisation of some and privileging of others. In relation to internationalisation in particular, frames that allow universities to win internationalisation competition establish group lines between home and international students because the latter do not get to be represented as equally qualified 'knowers'. They don't have to be, as in order to do well in the internationalisation category, universities do not need to present them as such; what they are instead encouraged to do is to pump up their international recruitment. International students' intellectual contribution is therefore dehumanised, invalidated and goes unnoticed in the university governance mainstream. So, if there is a systemic ground that causes epistemic injustice, then surely, and by extension, reciprocal integration in the process of the production of knowledge should be a systemic cure. For only when the cure is systemic, the oppressed can gain the credibility they deserve in the eyes of the oppressors, changing the distortion of who they are that has occurred with history.

And the final point is that when we have a ranking that supports university transformation towards practising epistemic democracy, university tutors will also need to act as 'radicals'. In that sense, the pedagogical intentionality encouraged by the proposed TEF metric is transformative for them, as well and represents, as explained in Chapter 3, a 'radical reform'. For too long university lecturers have been socialised into and complying with marketised imaginaries of international students, which have prevented them from entering into dialogue with the 'oppressed' and getting to know their epistemologies of knowledge better (Schartner and Cho 2017; Madge et al. 2009). Thus, the type of pedagogy that the proposed TEF metric can encourage is libertarian in nature, as it has the

8 Concluding Remarks   181

potential to transform the reality of oppression. It has been argued in the book that this type of pedagogy can cease monocultural teaching diets and practices that are based on coloniality. It can instead help to create an educational reality in which *all people are epistemic equals*. It also has the potential to develop a new understanding of teaching excellence—one which is constitutive of epistemic democracy as one of its key determinants.

References

Anderson, E. (2012). Epistemic justice as a virtue of social institutions. *Social Epistemology, 26*(2), 163–173.

Dahl, R. (2000). *On democracy*. New Haven: Yale University Press.

Foucault, M. (2002). *Archaeology of knowledge*. Abingdon: Routledge.

Freire, P. (1970). Pedagogy of the oppressed (MB Ramos, Trans.). New York: Continuum (published as Penguin Classics 2017).

Hayes, A. (2018). Nation boundedness and international students' marginalisation: What's emotion got to do with it? *International Studies in Sociology of Education, 27*(2–3), 288–306.

Hazelkorn, E. (2015). *Rankings and the reshaping of higher education: The battle for world-class excellence*. London: Springer.

Lee, J. J., & Rice, C. (2007). Welcome to America? International student perceptions of discrimination. *Higher Education, 53*(3), 381–409.

Madge, C., Raghuram, P., & Noxolo, P. (2009). Engaged pedagogy and responsibility: A postcolonial analysis of international students. *Geoforum, 40*(1), 34–45.

Marginson, S. (2013). Equals or others? Mobile students in a nationally bordered world. In S. Sovic & M. Blythman (Eds.), *International students negotiating higher education* (pp. 9–27). London: Routledge.

Naidoo, R. (2016). The competition fetish in higher education: Varieties, animators and consequences. *British Journal of Sociology of Education, 37*(1), 1–10.

Schartner, A., & Cho, Y. (2017). 'Empty signifiers' and 'dreamy ideals': Perceptions of the 'international university' among higher education students and staff at a British university. *Higher Education, 74*(3), 455–472.

Stein, S., Andreotti, V. D. O., & Suša, R. (2016). 'Beyond 2015', within the modern/colonial global imaginary? Global development and higher education. *Critical Studies in Education*, 1–21. https://doi.org/10.1080/1750848 7.2016.1247737.

Index

A

Agency 115, 125
Anglophone xiv
Anglophone knowledge 42
Anglophone position 41
Apolitical 42
Assessment of Higher Education
    Learning Outcomes (AHELO)
    x, 75, 79, 81, 83, 144
Australian plans 148

B

Bacchi, C. 6
Benchmarked-based standards xvi
Benchmarked-performativity 75, 76
Benchmarks 88, 111, 173

C

Changing the system 140
Classroom activism 132
Classroom community 22, 168
Collegiate Learning Assessment
    (CLA) x, 75, 79, 81, 82, 144
Colonialism 49, 51
Coloniality xvii, xxvii, 11, 29, 36,
    38, 40, 49, 52, 54, 56, 88, 98,
    105, 157, 169, 174
Colonial prescription 39
Colonial views 17
Commercial benefits 115
Commercialisation, of higher educa-
    tion 75, 180
Common Aggregation Hierarchy
    system (CAH2) 168
'Common good' agendas 35

© The Editor(s) (if applicable) and The Author(s) 2019
A. Hayes, *Inclusion, Epistemic Democracy and International Students*,
https://doi.org/10.1007/978-3-030-11401-5

183

184 Index

Conditional equality 49
Conditionality 49, 55
Consistency, in delivering transformation 86
Constructions, of international students 114, 134, 137
Cosmopolitan 80, 123
Critical pedagogy xiv, xxvii, 75, 89, 90, 93, 110, 118, 121
Critical relationships, with international students 14
Criticising, the TEF 109

Dahl, Robert xii
Democracy xi
  as relative concept 173
Democratic education xvii
Democratic equals xi
Democratic inclusion 22
Democratic participation, in classroom 15
Democratisation of knowledge 178
Determinants, of teaching excellence 63
Disadvantaging 13
Discrimination 10
Discursive practices xvi, 4, 9
Diversity 35, 142
Double-country oppression 40

Economic objects 32
Educational equality 66
Educational process 117, 121
Education process 112, 118

Emotions 12
Engagement 99, 100, 123, 140
Epistemic democracy xii, xxvii, xxxii–xxxiii, xxxvi, 49, 62, 69, 71, 177
  as determinant of teaching excellence 62
Epistemic development 22
Epistemic equals xxix, 31, 34, 141, 150, 174, 181
Epistemic inclusion 22, 121
Epistemic justice xxxi, 173, 177
Epistemic oppression xl
Epistemic silencing xl, xli
Epistemic violence 51, 53, 56
Epistemological privilege 53, 57
Epistemological silencing 60
Epistemological violence 54, 70
Equally qualified 'experts' 156
Equal participant 142
Equals xiv, 159
Equivalence of international students 115, 120
Espoused values 76, 96, 98
Ethical questions 117
European xiv
'Excellence' assessment 95
Excellence in teaching 76, 78, 80
Exclusion ix, 3
Experiences of home students 134

Faculty's engagement 124
Foucault, Michel 4
Freedom from coloniality 179
Freire, Paulo xiv, 89, 90, 99

Fricker, M. 68
Full-cost policy, for overseas students
32

H

Hard-outcomes 123, 142
Hegemonic system xviii
Hermeneutical injustice 68
Home perspectives as normative 121
Home students xiii, 115, 125
Home students' agency 169
Hostile environments 141

I

Immigration 33
Imperial echoes 29
Imperialism xi, 178
Inclusion 6
Inequality 3
Inter-cultural interactions 155
    and teaching, relationship
        between 156
Intercultural programs xvii
Interculturality 58
Inter-epistemic dialogue 62
Internationalisation xi, 14, 30, 50,
    77, 119, 134, 136–138, 140,
    144, 156, 157, 177
International students recruitment
    14
International students' constructions
    179
International Students' Survey 122

L

League tables 141, 144
Level 2 of the Common Aggregation
    Hierarchy system (CAH2) 165
Liberating the international students
    xxviii
Liberating nature 125
Liberation 22

M

Marketisation xviii, 112
Marketised pressures 105
Measuring and Comparing
    Achievements of Learning
    Outcomes in Higher
    Education in Europe
    (CALOHEE) x, 75, 79, 81,
    84, 144
Metrics x
Microaggressions 8, 11
Mignolo, Walter 49
Model, The 158
Monocultural diet of curricula 37
Moral questions 117
Multilevel regression analyses 143
Multiversities 77

N

National policies 141
National Satisfaction Survey (NSS)
    107, 110
National Student Survey (NSS) 133,
    135, 136, 138
National Survey of Student
    Engagement (NSSE) 147

186   Index

Nation state 80, 178
Nature and scope 140
Nature of analysis 143
Neo-liberalism xviii
New TEF metric 140
Non-Anglophone xvi
Normative contents and structures
134

Oppressors xvi
Othering 12
Outcomes x
Outdated representations, of international students xxvii

Pedagogical intentionality xvi, 42, 173
Pedagogies xv
Pedagogies of reparation 22, 92
Performance 78
Pietsch, Tamson 50
Plurality 16, 35
Plurality of knowledge 109
Policy 3
Policy a power xviii
Policy as Power 3
Policy effects 41
Policy hegemony 97
Policy representations, of international students xiii, 29, 157
Politicised 41
Power relations 12, 22

Prestige, of the British education system 31
Problematisations, of international students 115
Process standards xvi, 76, 86
Provider's submission 109
Public policy discourses 178

Quality of teaching xi

Radical reform 69
Random effects 166, 171
Random intercept cumulative model for ordinal data 161
Rankings xvi, xxxix, 61, 84, 98, 111, 179
Realisation of students as 'epistemic equals' xvii
Reciprocal democracy xiv
Reciprocal dialogue 179
Reciprocity xxviii, 132
Reconceptualisation, of outcomes 105
Regression model 171
Relationality xvii, 23, 41, 82, 174
between inclusion and pedagogy 150
Relational nature 136, 143, 167
Relational outcomes 143
Representations, of international students 32, 34, 120
Routine normalisation 16

Index

S

Sanctioned ignorance 56
Self-interpretations 9
Sense of belonging, to course community 158
Social change 78
Social complexity, of engagement 143, 148
Socio-political contexts 13
Spivak, Gayatri 49
'Split' categories 133, 137
'Splitting' the key NSS metrics 146
Split metrics 94
'Split' NSS metrics 170
Structural indicators, of levels of internationalisation 78
Student engagement 124
Subordination, of international students xiv, 15, 16, 169
Superiority, of the British education 30
'Supplementary' metrics 156, 168
Systemic change 131, 157
Systemic hegemony xvii, 76
Systemic injustices 180
Systemic international students 157
Systemic problem xvii

T

'Target' standard 173

Teaching excellence ix, 62, 93, 96, 110, 134, 138, 140, 144
measuring 111
Teaching Excellence Framework (TEF) x, xiii
Teaching process xv, 147, 174
Teaching quality
as consistency in delivering transformation 77, 88
as transformation 100
'Teaching standards' 172
TEF metrics 107, 155
Testimonial injustice 68
Thresholds 94
Transformation 86, 93–95, 173
Transformational quality, of teaching 96

U

UK Engagement Survey (UKES) xv, 132, 138, 139, 155, 158
United Kingdom (UK) xiv
University rankings 141

V

Value-added 113, 125, 145–147
Value for money 171
Value of international students 119

Printed in the United States
By Bookmasters